From Graduate to CEO

A Step By Step Guide to Career Development and Success

Samuel Ardley & Keith Coutinho

© **Copyright 2021—All rights reserved.**

The content contained within this book may not be reproduced, duplicated or transmitted without direct written permission from the author or the publisher.

Under no circumstances will any blame or legal responsibility be held against the publisher, or author, for any damages, reparation, or monetary loss due to the information contained within this book, either directly or indirectly.

Legal Notice

This book is copyright protected. It is only for personal use. You cannot amend, distribute, sell, use, quote or paraphrase any part, or the content within this book, without the consent of the author or publisher.

Disclaimer Notice

Please note the information contained within this document is for educational and entertainment purposes only. All effort has been executed to present accurate, up to date, reliable, complete information. No warranties of any kind are declared or implied. Readers acknowledge that the author is not engaged in the rendering of legal, financial, medical or professional advice. The content within this book has been derived from various sources. Please consult a licensed professional before attempting any techniques outlined in this book.

By reading this document, the reader agrees that under no circumstances is the author responsible for any losses, direct or indirect, that are incurred as a result of the use of the information contained within this document, including, but not limited to, errors, omissions, or inaccuracies.

Table of Contents

Introduction 1
Chapter 1: Choosing Who to Work For 3
Chapter 2: The Application and Interview Stage 14
Chapter 3: Understanding the Hierarchy and Business Etiquette 39
Chapter 4: Building Your Network 54
Chapter 5: Seizing Opportunities and Controlling Your Personal Development 62
Chapter 6: It's Time to Step Up—Management 80
Chapter 7: Managing Politics and Influencing Others 97
Chapter 8: The Leap to the Boardroom 105
Chapter 9: Defining Your End Game 114
References 124

Introduction

If you have ever wanted to get an overall 360-degree perspective of business and how to make a distinct impression from the moment you step through the door for an interview, then *From Graduate to CEO: The Secret to Career Success and Becoming a Leader* is exactly for you.

Never before has there ever been a need for individuals to be empowered with this breadth of knowledge than right at this very moment. We are living in ever changing times when it comes to office culture, career opportunities and the ability to move up the steps of the corporate ladder. The work landscape is changing constantly, which is exciting news for those who are hungry for change.

Looking back, we both wish we had a flavor of the knowledge and experience shared within the book, when starting our careers in the corporate world. Now with several roles behind us, we want to share it with you so that you can be better prepared in your journey from graduate to CEO.

Throughout this book we refer to an array of perspectives within an organizations structure. We will focus on starting out, the things you really need to be watching out for, and what you can be doing that will give you the distinct advantage over all the competition—and let's face it, competition is fierce. In each of the chapters that follow, we will unpack information in nine specific key areas for you to be aware of.

Each chapter has been written especially with you in mind, to give you a competitive advantage, no matter where you are within your career journey. Throughout the book we will share with you examples and different situations to help you to begin to appreciate the different perspectives individuals take within business.

Chapter 1: Choosing Who to Work For

One of the biggest decisions you will ever make when it comes to your career and the course it is likely to take is choosing who to work for. Typically, there are two types of attitudes people take when leaving college or university, those who are under the misconception that you need to settle for whatever you can get, and those who believe they have the expertise to become a CEO from day one. Being honest neither are right, you must approach your career with a much more balanced mind. Yes, confidence in yourself is incredibly important, but this must be more than matched in hard work and the right attitude.

While you may be newly qualified with all the academic, technological, and theoretical knowledge relating to your field of study, it is still exactly that— only the theory behind what actually happens within the profession itself. When setting out to secure your first step on the career ladder, you may believe that you can apply what you have learned immediately, but the truth is that from one business to the next, recruiters and hiring managers will look far beyond the knowledge that you hold at the application stage. People hire people, not qualifications.

The basic framework will be the same, but company culture plays a big role in how business organizations are run. Adverts for the same job function at two different employers may come with job descriptions that are completely different to one another. But the big question is, what do you want from your career? Consider not only what interests you, but also what you believe you will enjoy and of course things you won't. Just to get you thinking about what to consider when choosing the career you want to pursue and specific businesses you would want to work for and would value:

- Work life balance
- An office environment
- Remote working
- Development programs
- External facing
- Group working

Applying Everywhere Is a Good Idea, or Is It?

So, who do you decide to send your application to? Do you just look up job vacancies online and begin applying to anything and everything that looks like it may be suitable? Put simply, it's not a good idea at all, but if you do choose to do it you need to make sure you invest the time to do a very good job of it. The approach to hiring has advanced rapidly over the last five years, online application forms are beginning to supersede the simple CV upload and multistage processes have been introduced with features such as video interviews. But before you even get to that stage, as it widely understood popular graduate programs have application numbers well into the thousands, so you must stand out. If you aren't beginning your career and instead you are looking for a career change the businesses you are applying to are not only going to want to know why, but also what transferrable skills you will be able to bring with you.

Submitting your CV everywhere and anywhere may seem like a great idea at the time because as they say, much like fishing, you are only going to get a bite if your line is actually in the water. The difference is whether you are trying to land a guppy or you are looking for that prize-winning swordfish instead. The amount of effort is virtually identical.

The dreaded E word, Experience. Do you have any? For many candidates, having no experience on their CV could send their application straight to the rejection pile. There seems to be a lot of questions suddenly being raised that you may not have even thought of as yet.

Let's double back a little and let me ask you what you did during your holidays while you were studying. Did you make a point of trying to do vacation work, or even better secure an internship? Even unpaid work holds a lot of weight when it comes to applying for your very first job. Here's what it tells the organization about you:

- You may not have a lot of experience, but you are willing to learn.
- You had the initiative to go out and secure a role to develop yourself.

- You have some understanding of how a work environment operates and how to act within it.

Stack this up against those walking directly out of college or university with no experience at all, no matter how your knowledge compares to theirs you will already have a competitive advantage.

Consider internships on offer during your vacations. Look for those that are closely aligned to the type of company you would like to end up working for. What sometimes happens during these internships is that the company seriously considers the process as an extended interview for a permanent position. They request feedback from management and other employees that you may have interacted with during your time there. If you have done everything right, you may already have an entry-level position waiting for you before you have even graduated. Can you see how important one simple decision to look for work or choose to spend it lying on a beach could be?

The networks you develop on the internship will be useful as well as those you have made in college, and those throughout your personal life. You should not be afraid to use these networks - your competitors and peers will.

Getting back to deciding where you want to work or whether you are prepared to settle, stop and consider what this says about you as an individual. Depending on your course of studies, you should already know who the key players in your industry are and what your ideal job would look like. If you don't know what this looks like just yet, then this is your starting point. Invest some time in your future by beginning research and identify key qualities that you would like your ideal employer to have. Here are some questions to kick off your thought process:

- What industry should they be in?
- Is there a subsector you would like them to focus on?
- How many employees should they have?
- Are you looking for a microenterprise, a local employer, national employer, or a multinational global organization?
- Where would you like them to be situated?
- Should they be able to offer you growth opportunities?
- Do you want them to be a listed organization?
- What sort of company culture are you looking for?
- Are you looking for compensation packages that offer full benefits or would you be willing to forego benefits for a company that offers equity shares or that could develop your career faster?

Are there any other benefits that you would like the business to offer you?

Understanding What Interests You

Once you have all of the above information written down and clearly expressed, it's now time to look at those things that really interest you as an individual. Well, this is what you are typically told to do at least.

The harsh reality is that most do not know what really interests them when they are choosing what career path to take. From school, some take a very direct path through their further studies to pursue a specific career, such as becoming a doctor. Many however, do not know what career path they would like to take when they leave school or even completing their degree. If this is you, consider some of your ambitions outside of your career and think about how different careers could support or challenge those ambitions.

Looking ahead into the future ask yourself, where would I like to be in a years' time, five years' time and ten years' time. Be realistic in your aspirations but aim high. Some important things to think about when considering your career development is whether you would like to manage a team, if you would like to be office based, would you want to progress to a c-suite level, how important is a good work life balance and finally would you ever want to run your own business. Of course, there is so much more you could consider, but these are some rather poignant factors which will influence the direction your career heads in.

Typically, it doesn't matter what you've studied. It would be impossible for every educational institution to be able to predict every single scenario within every business in the world, and academics largely have limited relevance to day-to-day experiences. For example, an academic may stress the importance of naming and applying models such as Belkin in your work; however, if you were to name drop academic theories into daily emails, most would start to get nervous about your practical experience. Your studies are important, but what becomes more relevant is how you can seamlessly apply them in the business environment without looking like you are answering an exam question.

This is part of the reason why you need to decide what "school fees" you're ready to pay and in what industry. Let's give you an example that you can try to work from. Imagine that you have studied toward a degree specializing in economics. Surely it will make better sense for you to look for an organization that is geared toward economics.

If you graduated with this qualification but you actually hated the economics component, this would actually open other avenues for you in business organizations that aren't terribly concerned by the area of specialty but are really looking for the experience of working in a team and managing workloads. Suddenly you can shape your experience to support a role in operations or project management. Maybe you are interested in statistics, or the financial component. Look for those vacancies and then be sure to gear your application in that direction.

Many businesses are re-evaluating the way in which they hire young talent, considering shifting their recruitment focus from graduates to those coming straight from school. There is a wealth of research that breaks down the pros and cons of this move, however from a future employee's perspective it just provides you another route to start your career on. Remember,

University is no longer a must, especially with the rapid development of apprenticeship schemes.

In the following section, we are going to discuss the job application process in great detail. For now, understand that it's important to find a job that excites you. You may not realize it right now, but from the day you graduate until the day you retire, your happiness in the workplace is completely within your own hands. You and only you are in the driver's seat toward being happy. You are also going to be spending most of your life in the workplace—you may as well be sure that you're happy in your environment.

External Services Like Glassdoor and LinkedIn

Today, online services such as Glassdoor and LinkedIn are only becoming more relevant and important. What value are they able to bring to the party that you can't find out simply by Googling the business organization? To answer that question, there's a big difference between taking the company's website and a true reflection of the organization, warts and all! You want to know both the good and the bad. No company is likely to be that transparent online about themselves, after all they want to give their customers, clients, competitors and employees the best impression.

Every business organization wants to promote themselves in the best possible light. That's why they pay marketing and advertising agencies. Ultimately, they need to reflect only the positive attributes of a business organization. Let's closely examine what Glassdoor and LinkedIn can do for you.

Glassdoor is a hiring platform, but it is way more than your conventional online job board. They have taken the business of sales and marketing, recruitment, human resources, and honest analytics and feedback all rolled into one. This means that the critique or feedback you can read concerning a business organization is unfiltered. The site provides you with demographics and comparative tools for you to use to determine your salary scale. As if this wasn't enough, this platform offers interesting information and articles regarding businesses and what's happening in different companies. It gives you the ability to get the inside scoop before attending an interview and realizing that you don't really want it for reasons such as the cultural fit not being right.

LinkedIn has always been a business networking social media channel, but it is also used extensively to support recruitment and headhunting more openly. In each of these instances, some of the most important things you need to consider is that your information is regularly updated. Whenever you receive a promotion or an accolade, add it to your LinkedIn profile. What you need to realize about LinkedIn is that it isn't your conventional social media channel nor is it simply your CV. Prospective employers may look at your LinkedIn profile to find out more about who you are, as well as the professional interests and posts that you want to be affiliated with. All images and information on LinkedIn should be accurate and up to date. Remember, recruiters will look at your LinkedIn so portray the best and most rounded image of yourself possible.

You can add a banner to your LinkedIn profile that says "Open to Work which indicates to recruiters and your network that you may open to opportunities. LinkedIn can also work on matching your profile with potential vacancies – make sure your job search settings and filters such as job title, level and location are up to date and check it often. While we are going to discuss CVs in the next section, don't forget that your 'Experience' section on linked in should be accurate and up to date with details of paid and unpaid work experience. Finally, don't forget that the 'About' section is an opportunity to highlight your key attributes and aspirations to a potential employer. Make sure it's a reflection of who you are and where you want to be. Remember what we highlighted before, people hire people.

Internships

We have touched briefly on internships. We cannot stress enough how valuable these are when it comes to adding some meat to your CV/Resume, especially while you are still studying and you are trying to break into the marketplace for the first time. Not only could an internship lead to a permanent job role upon graduation, but being able to describe the experiences you had to future employers will be priceless.

Naturally, despite having internship references to add to your CV and your actual job portfolio, if you didn't enjoy your time with the business organization during your internship and you're offered something permanent with them, you should decline the offer. Your early career is as much about finding out the types or roles and organizations you are not interested in, as it is those you are offered. You will also enable someone else to be hired who may be better matched to the organization or role. Always be polite and appreciative even if you're declining a role. Later in your career you will see that however large your chosen industry is, your reputation and personal brand is important and every interaction has the potential to be remembered in the future.

For your industry, there may be more specific channels that are used, for example Twitter or YouTube. You need to ensure all social media out there presents the image you want an employer to see. If it doesn't, change the privacy settings to the videos of that Stag or Hen party. I have personally seen four colleagues let go for questionable personal posts made on Facebook that they thought no one at work would see.

Chapter 2: The Application and Interview Stage

Understanding the Recruitment Process

Let me explain to you why the recruitment landscape has changed so drastically. It's all about numbers. There are more people currently unemployed than ever before. This skews the recruitment market and tips the scales in favor of employers. They can virtually pick and choose those individuals they would really like to be working with.

Recruiters can receive in excess of 200 CVs daily per vacancy advertised on a standard online platform. This can easily equal about 1,000 or more applications per day. Therefore you will often notice there's a little disclaimer at the bottom of advertisements that states something to the effect that "should you not receive feedback within the next 14/21/28 days, please consider your application unsuccessful." All that this disclaimer does is cover the recruiter for not communicating with you once you've applied for several positions.

If that's the number of CVs your average recruiter is receiving daily (and these figures are actually on the conservative side), then take a guess how much time they have to go through your actual application. If you guessed several minutes, you would be incorrect. You actually only have a few seconds to make a good enough impression on a recruiter for them to sit up and take notice of your application.

It all boils down to a couple of seconds. A good recruiter (whether working in an agency recruitment environment or in-house for the actual organization itself) should be able to scan a CV within about 10 seconds and make a decision as to whether or not they are going to process your application. There's really no such thing as being able to make a good impression the second time around. This is why executive recruiters, headhunters and in-house recruitment professionals are generally so good at what they do. Don't think this is any different for graduate or apprenticeship schemes, applicant numbers for highly regarded programs are typically even higher here.

In this section, we are going to specifically discuss the application process as well as the interview stage with loads of vital tips and hacks that you can use immediately to improve your chances at landing that dream job. Given the sheer volume of documentation that both agency and in-house recruiters go through daily, it's now understandable why some of them behave the way they do.

The information we are going to provide you with will give you that winning edge when it comes to your actual job application as well as things to watch out for during interviews, covering both the do's and don'ts. This information comes directly from an executive director of a recruitment agency who has more than three decades' experience in both in-house and agency recruitment.

There is an unwritten rule when it comes to every organization's dress code and how you should be dressing for an interview. Simply by going onto the company's website, you will more or less get a feel for what the staff are wearing. If the dress code is chinos and golf shirts, dress in a neat shirt and slightly formal trousers. If it happens to be jeans and a t-shirt, level up and wear chinos and a golf shirt.

Cover Letters

There are a couple of trains of thought when it comes to cover letters.

1. First, if you are going to submit a cover letter, be sure that it's not bland, boring and generic. Be certain you address it directly to the right person. Other information that definitely needs to be there includes the job title or ad reference number. Be sure to include your own email address, as well as a contact number.

2. Second, ensure that your cover letter is direct, to the point (even if you add specific bullet points), and highlights all the reasons why you are suited to the vacancy being advertised. This could potentially save the recruiter quite a bit of time scanning through a detailed CV to find the information that matches their job spec. If you highlight this right up front, what could

normally take them about 5 minutes to scan through (should they have the time), can easily be reduced to about 30 seconds.

Use your cover letter to highlight suitable skills and similar experience that you have that will be beneficial to your application. The secret to a cover letter is that it needs to be brief and to the point, selling you to the recruiter within about 30 seconds and allowing them to make an immediate decision whether they are going to meet with you or not. Remember to close your cover letter off with your full name.

CVs /Resumes

The full name for a CV is a curriculum vitae, which many individuals battle to spell correctly. Don't worry, the term CV is widely used in the world of recruitment. You may also use Resume which is more common in the US.

There are so many mistakes that applicants make with their CVs and we are going to try to highlight as many of them as possible. Remember that knowledge is power and if you already know what recruiters and hiring managers don't want in a CV, it becomes much easier to put a professional document together that meets their specific criteria. Let's start listing some definite things to avoid.

Ditch the cover page that usually just has the words "Curriculum Vitae," "Personal Resume," or

"Professional Profile." All that it does is add another page to what needs to be viewed or scrolled through.

Unless you are specifically asked to provide a photograph with your application, please avoid this. Some applicants submit inappropriate photographs on their CVs, which automatically disqualifies them in the eyes of the recruiter or hiring manager.

Remember that what they actually see becomes their perception of exactly who you are. Unless specifically requested allow your CV to speak for itself. Your CV will be reviews initially for less than a minute, a photograph is just a distraction from the message you are trying to convey.

Ensure that your social media privacies have been set and your LinkedIn has a professional photo of you. It is not uncommon at the second interview stage that the interviewer will look at your LinkedIn or even Facebook to see what kind of person you portray yourself to be.

Avoid choosing multiple fonts with a variety of colors. Your CV should represent who you are, but it's not a piece of art. If you happen to be a creative individual wanting to showcase some of your talent, do so in the form of attachments to your completed CV document. An ideal font is one that is classical, and easy to read—consider using fonts like Arial 12pt or Calibri 12pt. You can change up the sizes of your headings to 14pt and make them bold. More than this can be perceived as overkill. When a CV is too busy and the decision-maker (recruiter or line manager) going through this document comes across all the busyness of your application, they eventually just move onto the next CV, skipping over yours completely Make sure there is sufficient 'white space' which allows your CV to be easily read.

Ensure all your information is on your CV. Would you believe that people still submit CVs without their contact information? Due to high volumes of applications from candidates, no recruiter worth their salt has the time to go searching in their database or previous emails to determine where the CV originated.

Be sure that your email address is a professional reflection of who you are. Avoid ridiculous or unprofessional sounding email addresses, for example goodtimejoe420@hotmail.com or rabidmonkey@gmail.com. Always keep your audience and your career trajectory in mind when you are setting up these email accounts. Avoid anything that can be misconstrued as being pretentious or over the top.

There are many different viewpoints on references, our view is that unless you are specifically asked to include them, adding the line "references on request" will suffice.

Now that we've covered things to avoid, let's look at some things you really should have in your CV without overthinking it.

All relevant personal information. Depending on where in the world you are, there are various labor restrictions and laws governing recruitment and your right to personal privacy. I have found the recruitment process to be completely different in various countries. Do your homework to discover what major laws govern recruitment or labor practices in your country.

Depending on how many years of work experience you have, only work 10 years back. Should you wish to provide any information on your work history beyond that, simply state on your CV "information available on request."

There are several specific styles of CV you can generate. The first is a detailed or comprehensive CV. This will be however many pages it needs to be, and each position will produce information relevant to that experience. The problem with these CVs is that they can be particularly lengthy and recruiters tend not to read them.

The second way to attract the interest of the hiring manager or recruiter is through a skills-based version of your CV. Here, you would still list all of your personal information. Although this is usually done in a much smaller format, the information still needs to be there. Simply list your positions with start dates and end dates, combined with a separate list that details your skills or areas of proficiency. The aim with this document is for it to be as brief as possible. You are looking at approximately a one to two page document.

Make sure your CV is consistent with LinkedIn and that all breaks in employment or study have been explained, e.g. Sept-Dec 2020 was a career break to act as a carer for a family member through COVID. Most interviewers will look to focus on inconsistencies in continuous employment to identify potential issues such as employees that may have been fired or have a checkered work history.

Situational Questions

These are questions that will give the interviewer some indication of how you would possibly think, act or react given a set of circumstances or situations. Typical examples of situational questions should be answered with real-life examples. You can prepare for these questions by considering different situations that you may have been involved in.

- How did you cope with different personality styles?
- Give an example of when you worked under pressure.
- How did you solve a problem?
- How did you work as part of a multi-functional team?
- Faced with conflict, what did you do to resolve the situation?
- What did you do to try to correct a mistake that you wish you had never made?

There are many of these types of questions that you might be asked to answer in different aspects of the business. Depending on what department you are working in, the questions will specifically be targeted in that general direction. To prepare for these, think about various situations that you have been in before that will show your ability to resolve conflict, work with customers, cope with disappointment, make mistakes, take care of priorities, show leadership and a whole host of other competencies

The interviewer is looking for situational answers to assess who you are and how you respond. If you've never been in a situation that they ask about, it's best to be upfront and honest but offer a response saying how you would respond in a situation like that.

Online Applications—How to Stand Out

Applying for work has become much simpler because of the way the world works at present. Communication is instantaneous, and while this could be seen as a bonus for some, unless you are making the very best of all available channels out there, you are potentially doing yourself a disservice. How do you decide between the plethora of online recruitment platforms and other not-so-conventional ways of making use of technology to put your best foot forward?

Channels

We mentioned unique channels, one of which has only really emerged as an excellent business community and hiring platform over the last decade. If you're currently in business and want to be noticed, be sure to maximize the exposure that LinkedIn is able to offer you. Anyone in any type of business should have a carefully crafted message that's tailormade to the audience you are trying to communicate with.

LinkedIn is potentially a very powerful business networking platform. Considering the numbers, users on LinkedIn currently amount to about 675 million individuals. You can find more than 30 million companies on the site. However, you should understand the market you are applying to. For example, for a TM1 coder in the IT industry, it would be more relevant to have a strong presence with IBM showcasing your technical abilities, but it is likely the recruitment team will still refer to your LinkedIn page as part of their checks.

Recruiters use it as a headhunting tool, so it's well worthwhile ensuring that your profile is as professional as possible. At present, you have the ability to upload various projects and other portfolio information directly to the site.

Brevity

Much of your success with online applications is brevity. Stick with the point and be sure that your 'tags' are correct. Tagging will cover each of the skills that you have, the job titles you are looking for, whether you are looking for permanent or contract employment and possibly whether you're open to relocation. Depending on the online platform you are using, they each utilize tags differently.

Tags

What purpose do tags serve? The reason why tags have become more and more important is to sift the wheat from the chaff, so to speak. It allows recruiters and hiring managers to search for specific keywords rather than doing a broad-based search. If you consider that they're looking for the best possible match to a job description that contains very specific criteria, by typing in as many of the key words possible, they can narrow the search down from a sea of candidates to a manageable amount like 20. Out of those 20, they can begin to search even further based on whatever the hiring requirements are. Not having tags is like just having your application on a platform with no real purpose. For example, if you are looking for a role within an accountancy firm, a tag that is regularly search for is "analytical".

Notification Settings

If you seeking a specific job and have completed all of the above correctly, the next thing to do is to set notifications across the various platforms. Choose generic tags that are slightly broader than exactly what you are looking for and then begin to narrow it down. While aspiring for certain positions is a very good idea, if you do not have the actual experience, do not include a notification or tag indicating that you do. All that this is going to do is frustrate both you and the potential organization that's looking for skills.

Skill Settings

More and more platforms are honing skills and asking you to identify what level your skills are at. Let us explain this a bit further. For you to indicate that you have an 'advanced' or 'expert' skill level in any industry, you would need to have around five to 10 years of hands-on experience working at that level. If you have just left college or university and have only done vacation work for three summers, please don't specify that your skill level is 'expert'—not even if you scored a 4.0 GPA for a subject that is related to that skill. An example of this would be when it comes to negotiation skills. You may have been on the university debate team for five years. Learning how to debate is not the same as being able to negotiate in a boardroom. You need to accept and understand that you have to begin nearer to the bottom and work your way up within the business world before selling yourself as an 'expert.'

A lot of platforms will actually now give you a prompt and specify how many years' experience you require for each level. While it helps to be confident that you can learn to do something, there's a difference between that and being conceited, arrogant or unrealistic in where your skills are right now. And there's no harm in admitting that you're just starting out. There are a lot of business organizations out there who prefer to be able to work with fresh talent. They want to be able to shape you into their way of thinking, helping you adapt to their corporate culture. They may prefer this to someone with 10-15 years' experience who they may see as possibly set in their ways. So, please don't think that the news is really all bad.

Video Interviews—Guidance

We are all aware that the world of work is continuing to develop. Technology is being used more than ever before. This includes video interviews taking the place of what were once physical face-to-face interviews. These can apply from the outset of an interview process, from initial interview screening via live video streaming with an agency all the way through to a final interview process with the organization. Here are some helpful hints for working with video interviews.

The very first thing you need to do once an interview has been scheduled is to enter the information into your diary with a reminder so you don't forget or connect late – it's best to connect 5 mins early to ensure you are ready when the interviewer is.

Be certain that you have sufficient data or your internet connection is reliable. If this is not the case, find a suitable environment for this to take place.

Do your research about the company. This is vital because it will help you formulate valid questions without sounding ignorant because the information is already available.

Be sure that you will not be disturbed throughout the interview process. If you need to, find a room in your home and ask your family to leave you alone for the duration of the video call.

Be professional in your appearance. Dress as you would if you were physically attending the interview in person.

Be sure that the background is as plain as possible and that clutter is not visible.

Ensure your lighting is good enough.

Test your system before your interview, including any headsets, microphones, and volume controls you may plan on using.

Speak slowly and articulate your words clearly.

Wait for the interviewer to finish asking the question before jumping in with an answer. Think carefully before you answer questions; there may be a twist or something specific they are looking for.

Put yourself in the interviewer's shoes. They ultimately want something they can work with. Mirror their personality traits. It is as much about whether they can see themselves working with you as the content of the response to the question.

Be sure that you know the name of the person interviewing you and write it down somewhere that you can see it during the interview process. Refer to them by using their name, yet be sincere.

Write down some key prompts to experiences you want to cover on Post-its by the screen so you can respond while maintaining eye contact at the same time. You shouldn't have to rely on these as it may come across as a scripted response, so these should be bullet prompts only.

Keep a physical copy of your CV within reach. A common question will be to talk through your CV. This is a chance for you to focus on the experience relevant to the role. A good interviewer will try to help you answer their question so make sure you respond to the questions and comments they provide and not with a stock answer.

Always be honest with your answers

It is helpful to put yourself in the position of the interviewer. Despite having taken 100+ interviews, I have never had any training to interview and probably have several bad habits myself. Most first-time interviewers fall into the interviewer role as a result of someone leaving. It is important to pick up a professional rapport with an interviewer and understand their drivers. The interviewer themselves may be nervous about interviewing you if they haven't done many interviews before. There is no single way to give a good interview.

In-person interviews

One subtle trick I can share with you. The interview starts when you enter the business. That person taking you to the interview whether a PA or a team member will more often than not be asked what they thought of you. Make sure you speak to them on the way to the interview room, even if it's just to calm your nerves.

My best interview involved all the stars aligning, the PA who took me to the interview was having a terrible day and I could see she just needed to vent about it to someone as she took me to the interviewer.

I had researched the person interviewing me and knew he had very similar experiences to me in similar markets. I knew by reputation that his interests were the same as mine, and he'd even worked overseas in the same neighborhood I had. I held my head up high and felt comfortable with all the questions asked of me, giving clear responses.

I asked a final question about the impact that something I'd read in the news was having on the company, and he seemed suitably impressed that I knew the market. As I exited, I could see the next interviewee entering, head down, very nervous. I wished them good luck and they didn't even acknowledge me. I knew at that point I had the job in the bag.

So, what should you take away from this experience? Firstly, show respect to everyone you encounter, this isn't something to remember just for the interview, but every single day in the working world. Treat the doorman with the same respect as you treat your boss. Speaking to the PA some time later once I was in role, she told me that she was asked for her input on the candidates so had a hand in my hire. Something as simple as showing someone respect can take you a long way.

Secondly, spend time building an understanding of the person that is going to interview you. Most people have LinkedIn and you can learn a lot from a LinkedIn profile, make a note of areas of interest, even something as a short comment on the latest sports results can really break the ice.

We will cover several questions you should think of asking before the end of the interview process.

The Dreaded Assessment Center—How to Succeed

Over the last few decades, the assessment center structure has provided an opportunity for organizations to form a more holistic view of a candidate. Big companies want to know that you can meet a rounded set of their needs, wants, and hopes from a candidate. These assessment centers can be very long days, so be prepared to put in some real work as this is a lot more than just an interview.

Assessments are carried out to determine behavior, emotional intelligence (EQ), and in certain instances even intellectual quotient (IQ). Although IQ is not as important as emotional intelligence anymore because work requirements have changed, it may be necessary for certain positions to determine your problem-solving abilities.

Assessment centers vary significantly from business to business and role to role, so there is limited preparation that can really be done. However, please remember that these are long days so make sure you have sufficient rest the day before. Give yourself enough time to get to the assessment center without becoming too flustered, having time to compose yourself before you go in or even a short five-minute wait in reception can really set the day off in the direction you want it to.

Most of these assessments are behavioral based and multiple choice. Clear your mind of any and all distractions. You need to be able to focus on the questions being asked. Don't overthink or over-analyze the questions. The one that seems to spring out at you is usually the right answer. Trust your gut instinct. It may be challenging to complete, but the answers will be a true reflection of who you are. Remember that there are no right or wrong answers in these assessments.

The single most important thing is not to try to trick the system. The only person you will be doing injustice to is yourself in the long run. Behavioral based assessments are exactly that and can be manipulated depending on your level of self-confidence and what's going on in your life right at that moment. If you aren't in the best place when it comes to your emotions on the day you take this assessment, it will reflect in the results of the assessment.

Emotional intelligence assessments can seldom be manipulated if they work from a behavioral assessment perspective. You should really be looking at those that work from psychological levels that are several levels down from behavior. An easy way to imagine this concept is to think of an iceberg that represents emotional intelligence. What's above the surface is only what you are choosing to show the world. We all know that there's much more ice below the surface of the water. That's pretty much like us. There are multiple layers that we choose to show the world. Beneath the surface, there are many other things that are going on.

Recruiters will often use group tasks which focus on solving a specific problem to build an understanding of the factors noted above. These tasks are built to show how you would operate within a real working environment. They will be looking at how you engage with the different members of your team, do you give the opportunity for other members of the team to contribute, do you promote them contributing or do you just talk over everyone to make sure you point has the biggest impact on the end result? In my opinion, the best candidates are those that very quickly show a natural instinct to lead a team, and this certainly isn't the most vocal. It is those who are able to vocalize the task at hand, bring in all of the team members, keep an eye on the time to complete the task, designate roles and of course are happy to stand up and present their findings.

Companies usually make use of these various assessment tools to determine whether you are going to fit into their specific corporate culture and whether you are a fit for a team that they're hiring for. Occasionally companies may even request these assessments be done for internal vacancies that have more responsibilities or possibly even a management component. They want to be certain that you are the best person for the job.

The Questions You Need to be Asking

This is an extremely important section to pay close attention to. There are way too many applicants who are so excited to get an interview with an agency or a company that they don't plan properly for the interview. Every single interviewer that I can think of will always close an interview off by asking you whether you have any questions that you would like to ask.

Typically, most applicants say no or offer a very generic and pre-prepared question. The problem with not asking any questions is that the interviewer will almost always think that you have either not done your homework properly or you have no interest in working for the organization at all.

An exceptional candidate would replay a question mentioned earlier in the interview and ask a related question. This demonstrates that you have a real interest in the process and that you are calm under pressure. For example, the original question may have been given an example of a time you've dealt with an irate customer. The follow-up from you could be, "One of the questions suggested I may need to deal with irate customers. Is that a common problem and do you think there is scope in the role to help address change to the root issues?"

Your final question should be along the lines of, "Are there any questions you'd like me to clarify or provide a further response to." This should reinforce the strength of your answers with the interviewer or give you a second chance to provide clarity to any responses that didn't quite hit the mark.

If they haven't offered guidance at this stage, you can also ask, "So, if I am successful in this round, what would be the next steps in the process?" However, the interviewer should hopefully be experienced enough to provide this detail unprompted.

Do ask the correct answers if there were any technical questions you think you may have got incorrect and explain the logic of your original response. This shows genuine interest, which is valued as much as the right answer.

When you are ready to finish the interview, do ask about the next steps in the process and when you can expect to hear back.

Don't try to intellectually challenge your interviewer. I once had someone ask me a technical question that had no relevance to the role, which confirmed to me he was the incorrect candidate.

You could ask if there are opportunities for growth within the organization. Be cautious when asking this question so that you aren't perceived as someone who doesn't want to stay very long in the position that you are being interviewed for. Word your question in such a way that you can make them understand that you are asking for the future. This will give them the impression that you are interested in staying with the company for the long haul and you're not just there to use them as a stepping stone.

You can ask why the current position has become available. The interviewer may not choose to divulge this information to you. If there's a problem within the department, they probably won't discuss this with you because they won't want to scare you off.

You can ask them what the process will be moving forward from this initial interview stage. Once again, this will confirm that you are interested in working for the organization.

Questions to avoid asking at all costs

"How many days of leave come with the position?" This gives the impression that you're more interested in holidays than actually working.

"When are salary increases due?" You need to really prove your worth within an organization, and if you are hired, all this information may be discussed with you by someone in human resources or detailed in an offer of employment.

"What's the manager like?" Be extremely cautious as it may actually be the manager that is interviewing you. This question could be perceived to be a bit picky

"How much does the job pay?" or "when is the first pay cycle?" These are questions that either they will bring up or, if you are successful, the HR representative will negotiate with you after the interview. It is fine to share your expectation, but really it's better to have someone decide you are the right candidate and be willing to stretch their budget a little. Think about this from the interviewer's perspective: Do you really want your first impression with them to be focused on how much you get paid, or that you will be a fantastic skill and personality fit to the team?

Making a Good First Impression to Your New Team and Your New Boss

There are several things you can do to make a good first impression on your new team as well as your new boss.

Arrive at work early so you can get the lay of the land. Being at the office early in the morning usually gives you a jump start on the day, every day. Giving yourself enough time to avoid commuting issues or traffic also allows you to be at work on time. This sets the right kind of example for your team to follow.

I recall a manager we had recruited who arrived late on his first day. Whilst the first impression was eventually forgiven, it was noticed by the CEO of the company, and though this wasn't the straw that broke the camel's back, it was an indicator of things to come and that employee didn't survive their initial probationary period in the business.

While you're putting your best foot forward in your new position, it may take you a little while to get to know everyone. It may be a good idea to have a meeting with your team where you allow everyone a chance to speak, introducing themselves and telling you how long they have been with the organization and possibly what their long-term goals are.

This single exercise will provide you with a wealth of information. You should be able to gauge who is just coasting for the monthly paycheck versus someone who is completely loyal to the business (these will be the individuals who have long-term goals). Ideally you are looking for someone that you can see yourself mentoring or being your mentor. You should be able to tell who the leaders in your team are (those whose opinions/ views are trusted and followed) versus those who are timid and shy. Often you go into these positions blind where there's no handover of any description.

You may want to set up time with each individual in for a brief one-on-one, and you will gain a better perspective of how the team interacts as a unit by observing everyone interacting together.

Make initial contact with your own manager asking to get up to speed with everything and understand what actions are needed and how they should be prioritized. Find out how they prefer to operate when it comes to regular follow-up sessions. Do they prefer written reports, and if so, how often and what information would they like to see on these reports? Would they prefer face-to-face meetings? Once again, how often and is there a fixed time when this would be suitable to do?

Be sure that the foot that you put forward on your very first day is the same foot that you put forward every single day.

Chapter 3: Understanding the Hierarchy and Business Etiquette

"Politeness is something you owe other people, because when you show a little courtesy, everything becomes easier and better. But first and foremost, it's something you owe yourself."
~ Anne Holm

Every business organization is run according to its own set of rules, and what is correct business etiquette for one is not always for the next. An example of this would be an organization that specializes in the global financial industry. They will operate much more formally than and SME business would. So, how do you get a feel for each business environment? This is where asking questions, as we've just covered in the previous section, comes in.

Now That You're In, How Does a Global Business Function?

Congratulations on getting your foot in the door and making it into a large market-leading company. In this section, we are going to concentrate on how a typical global business operation functions. We will look at its different departments, various roles that department plays, and how to make serious decisions when it comes to working in any of these divisions.

Sales

A sales division within a global company usually consists of a sales director, sales manager(s), sales team(s), and then any supporting administrative staff. Depending on the type of organization, your managers could be referred to as sales managers or brand managers. Sales teams could be further broken down into internal and external sales. Internal sales staff deal with inbound and outbound sales, often brokering large deals with other multinational corporations and even smaller outfits. External sales staff are exactly that—they are out of the office most of the time, prospecting for business. The only time they are in the office is to deal with paperwork, attending meetings, or resolving problems.

Your typical sales department is responsible for meeting and exceeding sales targets that could be broken down into year-on-year budgets, quarterly sales targets, and further down into monthly targets. These targets are usually set up by executive management and will be closely aligned to their business goals for the financial year. Depending on strategy, the business will normally look at taking an aggressive approach to sales, or they may be interested in maintaining market share.

Let's use the automotive industry as an example for what a sales department could be responsible for. Let's assume that the business is planning on launching several new models throughout the financial year. Sales targets will be broken down according to each brand. There may even be a different brand strategy put in place by each of the brand managers.

While brand strategy would fall under the brand manager's portfolio, it is usually dictated by a global strategy. This would be established at the parent company that is responsible for international global standards. The sales director would usually liaise on an international level and then filter information down through the rest of the sales department as necessary.

Let's break this down further and consider a new product launch. The initial product may have been in the design process for several years before it is actually ready to go to market.

Once it is ready, the sales division will get involved with formulating a brand strategy. Things like brand name, pricing, product launch, logos and overall corporate identity would be discussed by the sales division. Some of these discussions and decisions would be cross-functional and the sales division would work closely with other divisions, such as marketing, operations, manufacturing, executive management, global head office, and then strategic external suppliers or individuals that can help bring a product (vehicle) to launch successfully.

There are a lot of steps that need to be completed between the decision to launch and the actual launch because it isn't the responsibility of any one single individual to attend to everything. Sales will often work in close cooperation with marketing.

One thing you never learn at school is how vital a salesperson is to the business. If you become responsible for a key relationship with a client, you are able to be paid more than many senior executives with a simpler remit. Once you get to this level, you may be able to effectively write your own terms for salary, how you want to work. For example, in past employment, I know of one sales leader who negotiated down to working one day a week but still achieving the same bonus as they did while in full-term employment. This would never be accepted in another function and was achieved because they managed a key relationship with a client.

Marketing

Marketing as a division is fairly structured and has definite job-specific functions. This division is also usually led by a marketing director, marketing managers (who oversee specific products), and key account managers—this is almost a crossover function between both sales and marketing. They are usually responsible for working with key customers to ensure they experience the best possible service delivery.

Customer service agents deal with customer service queries, complaints, resolving problems, and ensuring that customers receive the very best possible service delivery from the business organization.

The marketing department could also consist of graphic designers, website developers, search engine optimizers, social media and content managers, copywriters, editors, marketing coordinators, merchandisers, advertising specialists, and so on. Many of these latter positions are relatively new since they have become necessary as social media marketing has exploded.

Sales and marketing work hand in hand to ensure that a shared vision is achieved and, where there happens to be corporate identity, that these standards are adhered to strictly. What do we mean by "corporate identity," or CI? This is your formal product branding. You can think of it in terms of the Nike swoosh, the McDonald's golden arches, and any taglines. Nike's tagline is "Just Do It!" Think of every brand you can possibly imagine. Every one of them has a specific font that their logo has been designed in, their brand consists of a specific color (think Virgin RED), and the list is hardly exhaustive because new brands are being released daily as new companies are formed. What would Amazon be without their smile?

Finance

Finance divisions cover a number of areas.

Accountants. These are broken down into two types—accountants that look at how the company has performed historically (statutory accountants) and accountants who look at how they can shape future performance with leadership (management accountants).

Cash and debtor management. This is the team involved in getting the money from clients into the business. It will involve negotiating credit terms, reminding clients when bills are due, and dealing with legal actions where debts go unpaid.

Purchase ledger, expenses and payroll. These teams are involved in making payments to people in a reasonable time frame.

Taxation team. Technical accountants who deal with returns to the tax authorities to ensure the correct amount of tax has been paid in relation to the company performance (In the case of Amazon, apparently this involves next to no tax being paid!).

While your career may not intentionally take you down a finance route, it will be important for you to understand a corporate balance sheet and income statement.

I cannot hope to explain the full detail of financial statements in this book. Accountants train for many years on this, but the highlights are as follows:

Income statements—these are a view of how much notional money or profits the business has made within a period. It looks at the sales less the cost of sales and associated expenses. This is where management tends to be focused as it is what affects an in-year judgment of performance and bonus awards!

Balance sheets—this holds a view of a business's assets and liabilities, including what investments the business has made for the future and how much debt they have accumulated in order to do it. Generally, balance sheets do not get the focus they deserve with leadership teams who remain focused on income statements. You can see this every time a new CEO is appointed as this is normally followed by a significant "write-off of assets," such as IT investments, to enable a return to profitability.

Internal audit and external auditors may also form a part of finance. The role between them is to ensure adequate controls are in place to mitigate operational and financial risks. They normally do this by testing the controls in place such as SPOE (second pair of eyes reviews). Internal auditors are generally concerned with managing risk within the business for the benefit of the board and shareholders, whereas external auditors are there to give an independent view that the financial statements (cash flow, balance sheet, income statement) are materially reflective of the financial health of the business.

Operations

Operations are the heart of a business and deliver the service or products that other teams have sold. The roles tend to be less glamorous than sales roles as they deal with day-to-day issues. The individuals that tend to succeed in this environment are very level-headed problem solvers.

Operations could be anything from the logistics of the business to manufacturing. The structure of operations would look something like an Operations Director with Operations Managers reporting directly to them. For example, in a manufacturing environment, you will have production managers, various line managers, electricians, boilermakers, mechanics, product developers, product support staff, logistics, delivery coordinators, dispatch clerks, pickers, packers, warehouse managers, and administrators.

Information Technology (IT)

This may have an IT Director with IT Managers reporting on all information technology related issues. Below them are IT programmers, IT product support, IT developers, IT customer support personnel, troubleshooters, installation experts, procurement specialists, administrators, and customer support personnel.

Human Resources

The Human Resources Director oversees the entire human resource strategy and code of conduct throughout the business, including all policies and procedures. They are responsible for ensuring that all policies and procedures are in line with government labor and employment laws and regulations. They are also responsible for permanent employees and temporary, contract and casual labor.

Human resources are responsible for ensuring that all disciplinary procedures are followed correctly and in line with the law governing the region. They're also responsible for the organizational development plan.

This needs to be drawn up indicating how the organization is structured, who is in what department, and who reports to whom. Very often, this is generated as a flow chart. It's a great way to get an overall view of the organization at a quick glance.

HR should ensure that all the latest trends in human resources are followed and communicated to all other departments. This is not just limited to external rules and laws that govern the country, but also any internal organizational laws that may be put in place from time to time.

The HR Manager is in charge of overseeing all junior human resource personnel. They may be responsible for many of the administration functions within HR, including but not limited to, taking on new staff, all administration and documentation that's required by law. This would include identity documents, banking information, tax documents and so on.

They generally handle end-to-end recruitment (through Recruitment or 'Talent Acquisition' teams) managing the hiring process from the initial advertisement all the way through to the offer of employment. For those applicants who were unsuccessful, they may make contact with them to decline their applications. This could be done by phone or email. Most large organizations have an internal and external hiring process where they have to advertise their vacancies internally first before they can consider applications from outside the company.

They usually handle the induction of the new employee into the organization, which means showing them around, making them feel comfortable, and introducing them to key members of staff. This is known as onboarding. Each member of staff would have their own personnel file with all this confidential information that's managed by human resources.

The Recruitment Manager is responsible for drawing up all recruitment policies and procedures and ensuring that all recruitment staff reporting to them understand them and are working according to them. Because you are working with people's confidential information, there are always a lot more rules regarding working with this type of information than you would have in other departments in the business. They manage a team of recruiters in house or may be responsible for communicating with and managing relationships with third-party service providers. This would mean ensuring that service level agreements (SLAs) are adhered to in line with the organization's needs.

Should there be an internal team of recruiters, the recruitment manager would be responsible for their training, managing their motivation levels as well as dealing with any disciplinary matters in the same way as all other departments.

Training Managers and trainers are responsible for all internal and external training within the business. This would depend on the outcome of needs analysis that were performed for individual members of staff or entire departments. A needs analysis would show where there were possible skill shortages that existed in various departments. Training would then be arranged to ensure that these gaps were covered.

The training division or training team would work closely with personnel to ensure that career aspirations were being met. They would be responsible for any internship or mentorship training programs within an organization depending on the needs of management in other departments.

It is all about strategic planning and succession planning with human resources. They need to be on top of their game to determine whether these plans are in place and they are being adhered to. They would also be called in to resolve any personnel issues, warnings, or disciplinary requirements whenever the need arose.

Line Managers and Matrix Managers

Line managers are your direct managers and the boss you are likely to interact with on a day-to-day basis. They will deal with performance/personal issues as well as your compensation and rewards. Historically, businesses have run with line managers as the solution to deal with staff. For example, in McDonald's, the person in charge of hamburgers in a branch reports to the duty manager who reports to the branch manager.

In more complex organizations there is often a need to manage the business in a number of ways. For example, to extend the burger scenario the person in charge of hamburger cooking may report to the branch manager. but he may also report to the quality control manager.

In a modern business, the way this is most likely to manifest is a role where you have a product class, e.g. burgers and a geography manager e.g. branch manager. While you may be worried about the practicality of this in terms of conflicts, these conflicts are healthy in ensuring sensible decision-making.

In a real-world example, I currently have six managers, two heads of functions, two heads of geography, and two heads of products. With corporate structures and expanding businesses, this is something you will have to adapt to.

The key here is that they are all important stakeholders to manage upwards to ensure functional decision-making. You can use them to your advantage to create allies to help get the right decision made, however it is vital to recognize and manage these relationships. Your career can be boosted or restricted by any one of these stakeholders.

Building Professional Relationships

One of the things that is extremely important when it comes to starting at a large multinational organization is the professional relations you can build. We suggest that you spend the first few days getting to know who all the key leaders are within the business organization. Decide what you are looking for in terms of your strategy growth and development within the business.

Then look at who will be able to help you get there (in terms of managers).

Who do you think you would be able to approach to possibly be a mentor? Will they be prepared to help you move up the rungs of the corporate ladder? How can you build better relationships with these business professionals? What opportunities are there for you to make professional connections with these individuals? Are there others you can rely on within the business who can possibly act as an intermediary where they can introduce you to each of the individuals you've identified as being able to assist you?

A lot of young people that are joining large organizations feel somewhat intimidated by senior leaders within their organizations. However, senior leaders are just people and in most cases they are happy to take time out of their day to support new people within their business. Not only for your benefit, but also for theirs. They will want to understand why you chose to join their organization and how they can improve it, to ensure they are able to retain the best talent. Of course, from the perspective of a new person within a large organization, having a network of senior "supporters" is only going to help you progress your career.

Understanding Your Audience and Talking to Senior Leaders

Take into consideration who your target audience is. These are all business professionals that have worked their way up to get to where they are present. While they are incredibly busy individuals, they are humans and most relish sharing their experiences to help develop talent. You shouldn't appear arrogant when approaching them, but most will be very receptive to share their wisdom if you have a clear vision of what you want to learn.

They have run the gauntlet in the business world and survived, coming out the other end much stronger than they originally went in. Each of these managers that are where they are today have a story to tell. If you could spend just five minutes with each of them, asking them to give you their single biggest piece of advice, can you imagine the goldmine of information you might be able to glean from this singular experience? Whenever you are communicating with them, take this into consideration showing interest in their experiences and respect for sharing them with you.

You are just starting out and are likely to be making many of the same mistakes that they made when they started out.

You should always remember, like your parents they themselves are not infallible, learn from their experiences, keep them allies and where you think appropriate adapt their lessons to your life.

Do try to ensure you use them appropriately as a resource. For example, you would get short thrift if you asked a CEO how to print something to the local printer... but you would get more recognition &

engagement if you were discussing how you are have responded to a customer and seeking their advice.

Chapter 4: Building Your Network

"Networking is not about just connecting people. It's about connecting people with people, people with ideas, and people with opportunities."
~ Michele Jennae

In this section we are going to cover the importance of having a network, why you need it, and how you can begin to develop one starting today.

Why You Need a Network

One of the main reasons for developing a network, especially at the beginning of your career in a large multinational organization, is to have the backup of individuals who will not only be there for you, cheering you on but who can act as sounding boards and mentors in diverse situations that you may find yourself in.

As an example, following the closure of a division in my last company with a genuinely talented team, four years on, I now have senior contacts in almost every relevant financial institution. By maintaining that network, not only do I have the opportunity to use my network to help keep up my industry experience, I also have multiple points of potential job referral for my next role.

The same will be true for you. Whist job boards, recruitment searches and advertised roles will be your primary mode of looking for a new role, it is your network which is likely to be more important in finding future employment opportunities either within your organization or outside it.

Building an Internal Network at Your Company

We discussed how to interact with management and strategic personnel toward the end of the previous section. The main reason for needing these individuals on your side is to begin building an internal network at your company. Start within the key division that you are operating within. Then approach others from departments that you have business dealings with. An example of this would be if you happen to work within HR. It becomes easy to meet up with or make contact with leaders and management in various other divisions.

Always approach them from a professional level. Explain to them what you want and ask them whether they would be willing to either act as a mentor or a sounding board when it comes to situations that are relating to their division. One of the main reasons you are doing this to begin with is to gain as much experience as you possibly can. You could start building this out it from a brief meeting with them every two weeks or even a monthly coffee meeting for 10 minutes. You will be surprised by what you can get done in the space of a focused 10-minute meeting.

Go prepared with a specific list of questions that you

would like to ask them. Some examples of these questions could be similar to the situational questions we covered right at the beginning of the previous section. Examples of these include:

Specific advice on how to handle a work situation (but anonymize people involved)

Advice on career progression and what skills they think would benefit you.

Advice on opportunities within the company or networks that may be beneficial to you in your career.

While the advice they will give you will be extremely valuable, more important is that will help build trusted networks and may help accelerate your career and open potential opportunities for you to develop.

Remember that you want to physically connect with these individuals. Otherwise, you could quite simply just email everyone, but that's not the point. You want to build relationships with each of these people. You want to be able to leverage them to assist you with building a network of other individuals who are not within your own organization.

Building a Network of People Outside of Your Company

Imagine what you could do if each of the connections you have within your own organization was able to give you just five names and phone numbers of people they either studied with or socialize with who may be able to help you—friends, neighbors, or other business leaders. Explain to them what your intentions are and ask them whether you can confirm with each of these people that they were referred by your current contact.

This is something that is referred to as a soft contact, compared to needing to go and hunt these people down cold, from scratch. It's always much easier to say that you were referred by "Joe Green, from XYZ." Chances are that these contacts will be more than happy to meet with you and give you a 30-minute catch up.

You can repeat this process as often as you feel you need to. By the end of each meeting, try to schedule another meeting that's no longer than 30-60 minutes each time. Leave sufficient time in between that you are not going to be troublesome with the person. Go prepared with approximately five questions each time. It's often a good idea to ask each of your network exactly the same question—that way you could get a range of answers, or you may see a common thread in the feedback that they are all giving you. That's when you know that the information you are receiving is paying off.

Be prepared for your internal network to be careful with who they introduce you to externally, they will be risking their own reputation by introducing you, be sure to always keep this at the back of your mind when engaging externally.

Joining Professional Networks and Attending Events

Another way of networking professionally is by attending conferences and events. Diverse industries often have annual conferences, business breakfast networking events, and other types of networking events. Keep an eye out for ones that are taking place within your area and sign up for several of these in a year. Networking at events is arguably the easiest way to expand your external network. Why? Many people attend conferences primarily to network with a certain industry, connections can be much more important than content.

What is really important about these events is that you don't go with the idea of just standing on the periphery watching all the action. These are known as professional networking events for a reason. They are meant for you to network. This means putting yourself out there, meeting others, introducing yourself, and stepping out of your comfort zone. It's easy to go into a networking meeting where you've been referred by someone, but when you go in cold, it's way more difficult.

Be sure that you have enough business cards that you can hand out and possibly a small notebook where you can make relevant notes of people that you are meeting at these events. Make notes as to what they do, where they're located, and possibly things that you discussed. You want to be able to refer back to this when you make contact with them again.

If you really are nervous about attending a networking event on your own, then make contact with a colleague and get them to attend the event with you. Be sure to tell them what your aims and intentions are. Let them be there to cheer you on and get you motivated to put yourself out there in order to get to meet those individuals who can help you in your career. Set yourself a specific target number of people you would like to meet. Don't stop introducing yourself until you reach your target for the day.

One of the most important things to do after these networking events is to follow up every contact with a personalized email and a LinkedIn connection request Refer back to your notebook regarding things you may have discussed and include this personalized information in your email. Thank them for their time and try to secure a brief meet and greet where you could possibly discuss strategy (similar to your 10-minute meeting with key personnel within your own company). Your aim is to get as many of these appointments as possible. Repeat the same process as you did with the managers within your own business.

Take notes, compare these and compile a list of actionable tips that you can use as an arsenal of tools to refer to whenever you find yourself in any given situation that you've been asking about.

Growing Your LinkedIn Profile

There are several ways of growing your LinkedIn profile. The first thing to do is to make sure that your

CV is complete, up to date, and in the LinkedIn format. This takes a while to do, but it is worthwhile at the end of the day. Next is to allow LinkedIn to connect with all your phone contacts and email contacts. You can decide who you want to connect to your LinkedIn account.

When you initially start off with LinkedIn, it will give you connection suggestions based on your work history, your skill set, companies that you have worked for previously, and individuals who you may possibly know. Once again, you have the opportunity to either connect or not. Remember that the point of LinkedIn is for business networking.

A way of growing your network is by regularly posting on the platform, but post things that are business relevant rather than personal information. There are plenty of social media platforms out there that can be used for your other interests. Be yourself but remember this is the primary way that potential employers, customers, and clients may view you, so maintain the professional image that you are comfortable with them seeing.

Join Communities

On LinkedIn, there are thousands of business communities that are relevant to the industry that you are currently operating in or interested in. Connect with those who have similar interests. When you connect with a business community, it is worthwhile following the community so you know some of the latest trends in the community. Belonging to communities allows you to connect with like-minded individuals who can point you in the right direction when it comes to looking for employment opportunities.

If you are interested in finding alternative employment, there are job boards for virtually every industry you could possibly imagine. Watch each of these job boards, and when you find something that you are possibly interested in, reach out to the person who can possibly assist you in being able to move your career forward. There are other important features that LinkedIn offers. A portfolio of projects can be uploaded, or you can ask for references from people you've worked with in the past. This strengthens your profile. Instead of others having to guess whether you have the capacity or capability to do the job, this is actual proof from others within your community, who give your CV and experience credibility.

Chapter 5: Seizing Opportunities and Controlling Your Personal Development

"Investing in yourself is the best investment you will ever make. It will not only improve your life, it will improve the lives of those around you."
~ Robin Sharma

In the following section, we will be focusing on another two important areas of business, the first being following through and making the most of networking opportunities.

Now That You Have a Network, Doors Will Open to New Opportunities

We've discussed the various different ways you can develop your network. If you make use of these contacts correctly, doors of opportunity can open. Some of these, you may not have even considered before. We're going to look at ways that networking can help you in your career.

It assists with building relationships with key people in your industry. By attending industry-specific events, you can not only keep abreast of what's happening with latest trends and developments, but also meet some interesting market leaders in the industry that you are in.

It helps you develop your self-confidence by forcing

you out of your comfort zone. In the previous section, we spoke about making connections within your industry; this however is talking about those things that you can learn to do that can serve you well throughout your career. Learning to approach and speak to market and even global leaders in the industry may just be exactly what you need.

If you happen to be someone who is shy at first, practice different approaches to people when you're first starting out. Polish these skills until they are well honed. Networking skills are some of the most important experiences you can develop throughout your career rather than just for here and now.

It doesn't matter where you are in your career. The mistake that many people make is assuming that you need to be in a certain place before you can network. This is a false assumption; you should be doing it throughout your career if you want to make the best out of almost every area of business.

Networking should be all about gaining additional knowledge from those you meet. Some networking events are cross functional and different industries are represented, not just the industry you're in right now. When this is managed correctly, it can open plenty of opportunities for learning. Seize each of these opportunities to learn about other things. Remember to reciprocate too.

Depending on who you are networking with, some of the conversations may mean sharing information about your industry. The only warning here is to be careful not to disclose any confidential information that you may have signed non-disclosure agreements on. They will respect you for it and you will find that they are also all about protecting their trade secrets. Open yourself up to the idea that these contacts that you are making should be long-term relationships that you want to develop with people.

Successful networking is never about how many individuals you manage to meet at one of these events. It's not like speed dating. What you are after are quality contacts and personal connections. By meeting fewer, yet maybe more influential people, it helps others begin to notice you.

Another benefit to networking is that it opens doors to you that to this point may have seemed to be tightly shut. According to LinkedIn, 80% of individuals polled found that networking was the key to success in their careers. Just one of the ways that this can happen is by providing the inside scoop to vacancies that are possibly not yet advertised.

Something you really need when it comes to networking is exceptional communication skills. These are often referred to as soft skills. Networking also means being brave enough to communicate with people from all levels within an organization.

Many of these events will be attended by key market leaders throughout the entire process. Be as professional in your communications with others as best you can. You want your conversation to be the one that sets you completely apart from the rest of the individuals there. The components in communication can easily be represented as follows:

Sender—this is the person who is delivering the actual message at the time. This is usually done through some means of communication.

Receiver—the person receiving the message through active listening.

Method—communication can take on so many different formats today. You could either be communicating face-to-face, via telephone (including cell phones), via email, professional or social media (non-verbal communication), or body language (also non-verbal).

Message—what is it that you are actually wanting to say? Do you have a specific thought process that you should be following that can make your communication with others more accurate and beneficial to you?

One thing about communicating with people you've connected with through networking events is that you should be getting to the point as quickly as possible without building too much fluff around it. Remember that many of these individuals will be market leaders and receive hundreds of communications they need to deal with daily. Make sure your email stands out, is clear, concise and has a call to action.

Make your communication as short and sweet as possible, sticking to the facts, asking for what you want, and then listening. At the end of the conversation, be sure to thank the individual for their time. Your message should be delivered as clearly as possible to avoid any ambiguity.

It's important to nurture each of these new relationships. Some of the conversations are likely to be mentally stimulating where you can share ideas with one another.

Other benefits include receiving advice on areas of your job where you might be struggling. This would come from others in the same industry as you who have possibly gone through what you are currently experiencing. Imagine the power of being able to call up someone and getting their opinion or insight into something that you happen to be battling with. Rather than doing it alone and going into a situation completely blind, it may mean that you are armed with enough information to resolve your problem. They've been there, done that, got the t-shirt, so make the most of it and lean on them for advice.

If you're not all that good at communicating with others, this will be the perfect opportunity for you to practice. If you happen to be shy, this will give you the confidence you need to be able to get out there and meet up with interesting strangers.

It's better to address this early in your career if you want to progress regardless of your role, you're going to have to overcome this. I used to be very uncomfortable presenting and get extremely nervous. I can assure you this is the same for everyone no matter how confident they come across and it does get better with experience.

Many of these interesting people may have the potential to assist you with your career. Some of these could be entrepreneurs and investors. They may very well be in a position to assist you with getting a start-up business off the ground. If they don't necessarily have the capital to back you up (if your idea is worth pursuing), they may know of other investors or entrepreneurs who are in a better position to do so, or they may be able to give you advice on where your plan is lacking. These individuals are excellent sounding boards when it comes to business, startups, and various other career-related activities because they were once where you are now. Remember that chances are that they will already have another network of like-minded professionals who they may be able to introduce you to within their network.

Networking will give you the opportunity of being able to connect with those who you could possibly approach to be a mentor, or various mentors depending on the specific area of business they are in. You may want to approach more than one. An example of this is if you are considering a start-up business and you don't know of anyone who has done what you specifically are trying to do. You can look for those individuals who have key skill sets in the various facets of the business organization, for example someone who specializes in finance and administration, an HR professional, and someone in marketing and sales. Each will have something to offer that's specific to their side of the business. Learn all that you can from each and combine all this information into something that will make for a fully rounded entrepreneur.

This allows you to help others. No matter where you are in your career journey so far, there will always be someone that is more junior than you. It's safe to say that you will be able to provide advice of your own based on your own experiences to date. Don't sell yourself short. Everyone can do with some help, even if this means that it's motivational.

Networking can lead to professional relationships that will last. These relationships can become even more than that, often proving to be long-lasting friendships that will stand the test of time. Many of these contacts can help you move toward your aspirations as you climb your career ladder.

Through meeting with others in your own industry, you can be provided with the occasional wake-up call in the form of a reality check. This would happen when you meet those who have been in the same industry for as long as you have, but they are either higher on the corporate ladder than you, or they've moved their careers forward at a much faster pace than you have.

Working for a company for a certain amount of time can lead to feeling complacent and comfortable. Instead of looking for opportunities and ways to grow, you prefer to wait for these opportunities to come to you. Unfortunately, life and work don't always work that way. You often have to be proactive enough to get out there and make things happen for yourself. Being in a position where you are reminded of what others have achieved can be one of the motivations you actually need to move forward with your career.

Building Confidence in Yourself

Being able to use your network you can fine-tune exactly who you are and develop your own personal brand. This helps define you and makes you different from everyone else. Often this is what sets you apart. It's also the message that you get to share with the rest of the world regarding who you are as an individual.

Believe it or not, networking can have a positive influence on who you are as an individual, how you feel about yourself, and how happy you are or can become. We've spoken about being able to improve your communication skills; this will improve your self-esteem and feelings of self-worth. Try to seek out those people who are like-minded to yourself. Connect with them and then make these connections work for you to your best interest.

Identifying Your Personal Skills That Will Set You Apart

What are some of the things that you are really good at that set you apart from the rest? Do you have finely honed communication skills or listening skills? Are you a creative problem solver, or intent on providing the ultimate in customer service? Whatever it is that is going to set you apart, focus on these skills because that will potentially land you another job.

Selling Yourself, Building a Personal Elevator Pitch

Before you can successfully craft a short elevator pitch about yourself, you need to clearly understand who you are, your strengths and weaknesses, and your achievements. Few of us are confident enough to brag about our achievements, but if you really want to be noticed, you will need to. This is a short introduction about yourself that you can get through in about a minute.

It should tell the person you're introducing yourself to exactly who you are without being long-winded or taking up much of their time. Remember that the key to networking is being able to meet as many key influencers as possible and deliver an initial and favorable impression. If you're planning on spending 15 minutes just introducing yourself, there will be so much that you will miss out on. So, what are some of the things you should be saying during this time?

Introduce yourself by name. What are your interests, passions, background and experience, and what do you do? All that needs to be cleverly crafted into a few sentences, under a minute. You need to leave a lasting impression, and the entire goal of an elevator pitch is to make others want to get to know you. You want them to remember you and form some kind of professional relationship with them. One of the keys to a successful elevator pitch is that it needs to be practiced over and over again so you don't get bored of saying what you need to say and switch off mid-introduction. You want people to want to get to know you more.

Getting a Mentor

From the network of business professionals you meet, seriously consider which of them would make for the best mentor(s). Remember that the point of having a mentor is that they have been where you are now, and they are currently sitting in a position that you would like to aspire to in the future. Having more than one mentor, as long as they are all adding value to your career, is only a good thing. Keep in mind however, you can outgrow a mentor and you should always be looking for someone who can develop you further.

Learn From Your Mistakes

In business, whether you are just starting out, sitting in a junior leadership position, or the CEO, we all make mistakes. None of us are perfect and it's part of being human. Some of the mistakes we make will possibly be life altering, while others are just like a simple blip on the radar, quite easy to fix or make amends.

There is a well-known theory on process improvement gained from the automotive industry called the "six sigma" approach. This involves repeating a process until you eliminate all but the remotest chance of repeating that mistake. It is the same concept that we apply generally to life like learning to walk or drive a car. The quicker we learn from our mistakes, the sooner we can move on and the quicker we can progress toward achieving our goals. Life is all about lessons and has been since the day we were born. When we resign ourselves to this fact, we will discover that there's way more out there than we could ever have imagined.

Go Out of Your Way to Learn More

Knowledge is power and it is only when you have this knowledge that you can apply it. You need to go out of your way to be able to learn as much as possible and gain as much wisdom as you can, especially in your area of business. As mentioned earlier, if you want to get a broad base of knowledge, it works if you go directly to individuals who have that information already. Here you can ask them first hand to provide you with situational examples, or you can ask situational questions.

Don't even be afraid of asking about a problem that you may currently be experiencing right now that they could assist you with. Too often, we are under the impression that because we went to college or university and we have a piece of paper neatly framed behind our desk, we now know everything there is to know about a particular subject. This is simply not true.

We will never be able to say that we have been able to absorb an infinite amount of knowledge. Instead, be humble and admit the fact that you don't know everything. This is one of the greatest benefits of networking and being able to make use of those around you. Many of them have years and years more experience than you do. They can help you by sharing what they do know, but only if it's something that you really want to learn. If you ask and then actually listen, you will be amazed by how much valuable information you can learn from others.

Attend Events and Speak to People

Other ways to learn are by attending events and speaking to people. Most events have market leaders as guest speakers, and just by sitting taking notes at these events, there's huge value to be had. Don't be afraid to speak with people afterward. Watch out for announcements on social media about events near you that may be happening. These are usually well attended and there are coffee and lunch breaks where you can get a good chance to mingle.

Developing Personal Resilience

Resilience is having strength to overcome obstacles and challenges. These will always be found in the workplace. This could be anything from equipment that malfunctions to interpersonal challenges. Being emotionally strong and capable of withstanding whatever is thrown at you is a surefire way of moving your career in the right direction. Resilience is having the tenacity to stand up whenever you get knocked down. It's not allowing obstacles to get you down. Part of the world of work and every career out there is the knowledge that there will always be things that can go wrong. The question you should be asking yourself is whether you have the mental and emotional capacity to be able to handle each of these things professionally A quick internet search or search on any podcast app will give you further hints and tips on this important workplace skill.

Navigating Change and Becoming Adaptable

Change is also always bound to take place in the world of work. Whether this is in the form of a manager retiring or companies merging, one thing is guaranteed: change will happen. Not everyone is a fan of change and it can indicate the fear of the unknown. Fear is a normal and natural reaction to change, but it doesn't have to be.

The solution to overcoming this fear is learning to become adaptable and accepting of change. It's being prepared to embrace it to see what new and exciting opportunities present themselves that you can look forward to. Changing your attitude toward these situations can often make the experience easier, and perhaps even career-building rather than challenging. Your attitude is something that you have control over, and you can choose this for yourself.

Pushing for Promotions

Another part of working for large multinational

organizations is that there are almost always opportunities for growth and personal development. Whenever you believe that you have proven yourself in your current position and there's nothing more that is challenging you, it may be time for you to look for other opportunities within the business. It's usually a good idea to seek out the advice of either those who are mentoring you, your manager or HR.

They will be able to tell you whether you are suitable for the promotion or not. Before going guns blazing at trying to secure a new position, double check that you tick all of the boxes. If you are 90% there and there are one or two things that you feel certain that you can learn within a reasonable time period, by all means submit your application. Where many employees make a mistake is by keeping their current position for only a short period and wanting to make a move into a much more senior role.

You may need to get quite a bit more experience under your belt before you decide that you're ready to move on. There are usually only a few reasons why individuals want to leave their current position, and only one of them is money. If you are battling to get along with someone within your department and you really don't see yourself ever being able to form an amicable relationship with them, then there's nothing wrong with approaching your manager or mentor with the view to a lateral move or a reshuffle of the department.

Once you have been with an organization for a reasonable amount of time and you believe that you tick all the boxes, it may well be time for you to climb that corporate ladder. Two things may happen in this instance. You will either be successful in your application or you won't. What is going to make a huge difference with regard to applying for future promotions is how you handle yourself if you are unsuccessful. Should you be successful with your application, the time will come for you to look at negotiating your package with either the manager, line manager or HR. It is important to take the promotions that are right for you and align with the direction you would like your career to progress in. Stepping sideways into a career path that offers a brighter future, is better than a step forward where you are.

Negotiating Your Compensation Package

It's important to understand that every single department runs off a relatively strict budget per annum. Part of this budget allocation will be for salaries and other benefits. The reason we are telling you this is that you need to be aware before you shoot yourself in the foot that a compensation package may not be as negotiable as you would imagine it to be initially. Most internal promotions will indicate what the sliding scale is between lowest to highest.

If you are driven solely by the short-term gain, you need to plan this right; understand the environment you work in, what you offer the business, and how you can monetize it.

Something to consider is that the higher the sliding scale, the more you need to be able to simply slot into the position and hit the ground running. Any organization would rather invest in its own personnel than have to look for someone externally. The main reason for this is from a cost perspective. Companies pay a large percentage to recruitment agencies or headhunters to find them the ideal candidate to fill a specific position.

Again, you should consider this from the perspective of your manager. Why would they want to give you more money and reduce how much they have to spend. The argument needs to be something that is compelling and that requires immediate action.

You should therefore always try to start negotiation from a position of strength. For example, imagine that you are instrumental to the delivery of an important project, or you are in the middle of or have just converted a sales campaign, or you have been approached by a competitor. In each of those situations for the manager, the cost of losing you is far more than the cost of retaining you, so financially it makes sense to react.

Hopefully, you can see from this just asking to be paid more because John, Jo, and Jane get paid more is a comparatively weak argument for the manager to consider.

If you can prove that your compensation requirements are reasonable and in line with your current skill set, qualifications, experience, and the value that you are able to offer the company, then more often than not, you will be in a better position to negotiate a suitable package. Do your homework first by looking at other organizations in the same market sector or industry that you are in to see what the job title or position pays on average. Finding this information is extremely easy via the internet.

Additionally, throughout your career you should work with your respective managers to develop development plans. These development plans are put in place to support you in developing in both the areas you need to improve for your current role, as well as areas that you believe will support you in driving your future career. Having a development plan in place can also aid the compensation discussion. Being able to retrospectively look back and highlight what you have achieved over the last period will only strengthen your case for a more compelling compensation package,

Glassdoor not only has specific industry information, but they can provide you with salary scales as well. All that it means is that you need to do a bit of homework. A word of caution when it comes to these negotiations—you don't want to oversell and under-deliver or leave money on the table. One of the best ways to negotiate would be to ask for a specific period of time where you can prove yourself in your new position at a set salary rate with a negotiated increase thereafter. Most organizations will then be able to tell that you're in it for the long haul, that you are planning on remaining loyal to them, and that you are willing to prove yourself.

Understanding When It's the Right Time to Change Jobs/Businesses

Once you feel you've exhausted every possible avenue and option for promotion or lateral movement within the organization, or any application for promotion keeps being blocked, it may be time to move on. You need to be certain within yourself that you are making the right decision, though, and you are not jumping from the frying pan into the fire. The timing needs to be right and you need to be sufficiently certain about your chances of success elsewhere before you do so.

Making the move into a new team or organization must also align with where you would like your career to progress to. If you are looking around you in your current position, unsure what else you have to learn, yet you feel like you have knowledge gaps, it may also be time to consider a move.

Chapter 6: It's Time to Step Up Management

"Management is efficiency in climbing the ladder of success; leadership determines whether the ladder is leaning against the right wall."
~ Stephen Covey

Ways You Can Move into a Management Role

We are going to look at several ways that you can move into a management role within a large organization without too much difficulty.

Internal Promotion

This happens when either a new role is created based on company growth, someone resigns, or they happen to be promoted. With an internal promotion, everything is handled internally through your manager, senior leader or your company's HR division. The internal vacancy is created and advertised throughout the organization. There is usually an expiration date for the submission of CVs and applications.

You should be aware most internal promotions are decided prior to any interviews taking place. No one will ever admit to this but it is common practice. Well before any opportunities arise, you should be sharing with your line and matrix managers your ambition within the organization and have allies who will endorse you internally.

After this entire process has been concluded, a round of interviews will be conducted by the division where the vacancy exists. This could result in a final shortlisting of candidates. Once a final shortlist has been achieved, there may be a third round of interviews conducted with the shortlisted candidates, depending on the level of the vacancy. The final interview may even be a panel interview with several of the top executives of the organization.

Promotion processes will vary between industry, Company and seniority so you should ensure you use time your manager to explore how these work, annual processes and timelines so that you can start preparation at the right time.

Restructuring

If your network is strong and you are technically able at your job, this is a possible opportunity to progress your career. The reason is that for the right person, they will design a job around you. In many instances, when restructuring takes place, management can sit with HR to formalize a job description for the "ideal candidate," but they are often uncertain of what the role is going to require in its entirety.

Recently a colleague was involved in a restructure, and coincidentally happened to know the restructuring HR partner. The candidate's role didn't exist in the new business; however, during each meeting the HR partner went to, the team would mention this individual and how they needed to ensure a job was found for them. This went on for a good couple of months whilst the design of the organization continued to form. Eventually it resulted favorably for my friend who got both a promotion and a more senior managerial role out of the situation. Although restructuring is never a pleasant process, in fact it can be incredibly stressful, change isn't always a bad thing.

The exact same recruitment process will take place from an end-to-end 360-degree recruitment situation. From the initial advertisements through to extending the offer, each step of the process will be followed through between HR and divisional management rather than just line management.

The restructuring of a department or organization can be a challenging time and you need to exercise personal resilience. However, for right person with the right skills, attitude, experience and network as we have already discussed, the opportunities can be significant. Even if restructure means that the organization changes in way you don't think is positive, remember to think about your 1, 3, 5 or 10 year career plan and think about what experience and opportunity you could take out of it to get you closer to your goals even if that is a different path to that you expect.

Your Manager Is Retiring

A rather old-fashioned way of progressing in a business

is to await the departure of someone else in your team. Like any internal promotion, it is important you make your ambition clear and get the departing employee (assuming they are leaving on good terms) to be your ambassador. This situation should seem very positive for you as an individual. It is a very rare chance to get a clear insight into where your line manager and company see your role in the business. If they don't give you a promotion and offer it externally, you should get clear guidance on why you didn't get the role and understand where your career is likely to progress if you remain with them, given they have indicated by an external hire, that your role probably won't be a direct promotion in the next two years. You can either leverage this to move into another area of interest or use it as a catalyst for change and look for opportunities outside your current organization.

Moving to Another Business to join or Lead a Team

It is quite possible to hit a glass ceiling in your current team where either the jump to the next level is too large or the remuneration jump is difficult for your manager to come to grips with. This may lead you to look for alternative options external to your organization.

Here, you're looking at an external hiring process. You may find that you're initially finding new roles through a recruitment agency and feel like you are going in blind (you have no clue as to who the company is). All that you have is a job specification. Be sure that you are able to tick off most of the boxes once again. Some agencies may be reluctant to disclose their client's name at before putting your CV through a first screening. Either way, you should ask and take notes about how they describe the Company. It is not unusual for a description taken verbatim from a Company website and a quick internet search can reveal a company even if the agency cannot. This recruitment process may or may not take longer than your internal vacancy process, or it can be pretty quick depending on the urgency of the vacancy and how quickly the recruitment agency and the organization operate.

Be prepared to jump through several hoops when it comes to this recruitment process. With a management or leadership position, you can always anticipate having to go through an assessment process. This may be handled with the recruitment agency or division already. You can expect a slight delay because some of these assessments are generated externally and take a while before they are submitted back to the agency or recruiter.

More and more organizations are moving their recruitment in house in order to save the money they would normally pay out on recruitment fees. This is completely dependent on the actual vacancy. If the position is highly specialized and the company has no intention of looking internally, they may take on the recruitment agency approach. When being interviewed by the recruitment agency, be as professional as possible.

Should you be shortlisted, be prepared to do your homework before going for your first interview with the actual company. Find out as much about the organization online as you possibly can. Once again, Glassdoor is a phenomenal resource that you can rely on for information. Utilize your network, search the company on LinkedIn to see if you have contacts there already and don't forget the company's own website. Here you may well be able to get enough information to know who you are going to be interviewed by, their name, and possibly even a photograph.

Interviews are the one time in life we would encourage light stalking via social media. Use LinkedIn to investigate your interviewer, understand where they went to school, if they spent time overseas, which industries they worked in… and use it to shape your experience to something that they can relate to.

You need to discover their address so you can do a trial run to their office at the same time of day as your interview. This will give you time to arrive there with sufficient time to spare. It's best to arrive early. In large offices this will help you navigate through busy reception desks and security protocol. Almost every large organization has their own set of internal documentation that they need you to complete. This will be completely dependent on their hiring policy. While you're filling this in, be aware that there may well be an assessment or two thrown in with the paperwork.

Dress appropriately. If you arrive at an interview wearing a three-piece suit and tie and the recruiter is dressed in a pair of jeans and a t-shirt, you are going to make them feel uncomfortable throughout the interview process. On the other hand, if they are a financial institution that generally still wears corporate wear, don't arrive dressed in a casual outfit. You want the recruiter to take you and your application seriously.

If you really cannot find out a company's dress code on their website, don't be afraid to give them a call to ask. Speak with the receptionist and explain that you have an interview with the company and you need to know what to wear. The receptionist is always the best individual to be helpful with this information.

You want to dress one up from the company's official dress code. If the dress code is semi-casual, go to the interview dressed smart. If they wear uniforms, wear a corporate suit.

It's Not Always Within Your Control, There Could Be Many Factors at Play

Being promoted within your own organization or even moving into another company may not always be in your control. For this reason, don't beat yourself up if your application is not successful. You can always ask a recruitment agency if they could provide you with feedback. Depending on who they are and how close their relationship is with their client, they may or may not be willing to provide you with this information.

When you ask for this information, approach it from a place of humility (a place where you would like to use this information to improve and grow) rather than a place of anger or aggression. Remember that every organization has their own set of unwritten rules. They may not be willing to disclose this to a recruitment agency.

Project Management, Successfully Managing Your First Project

Successfully managing a project involves more than just you. It would normally involve an entire team of individuals. Within your project, there will be things like project budgets that need to be adhered to. For a project to be successful, it usually needs to meet all the relevant project parameters on time and within the budget.

Projects usually have both internal and external stakeholders or different parties that have an interest in seeing the project being achieved. The timing on projects varies depending on the project parameters. This could be from a few weeks to several years and even decades. The longer the project, the more difficult it is to assess its effectiveness, but regular project analysis and reporting continues to take place.

To be effective as a project manager, you need to be able to manage people, resources, goals, communications with stakeholders, timelines, and the management of everything project related. One of the final parts of project management would be regular reporting to all relevant project managers as well as internal and external stakeholders.

In our experience, people are often asked to manage a project before they are asked to manage a team, and they are often asked to do this if they have performed well or have expressed the need for a way to accelerate their career or get involved in something interesting. This gives leadership the scope to assess management skills with a relatively low risk before offering a permanent promotion.

Project management is a skill in itself with courses designed specifically for it and it is well remunerated as a career; however, all the executives appear to have had hands-on experience in leading or delivering a project. It is almost a rite of passage to develop some of the skills you need for managing and leading.

People Management, Learning to Motivate, and Understanding That Everyone Is Different

Managing people depends entirely on who they are individually. It's understanding that we all bring something different to the party. Once you understand the difference, then you will be able to work with them effectively. In many ways, this is where sound emotional intelligence skills come into play where you utilize the people-awareness component to assess what type of personality you are dealing with. From thereon, your communications, management and motivation of each of these staff members will either help them flourish or cause them to be ineffective.

Being able to supervise people effectively is a vital skill

for successful managers. If this is an area where you feel you lack the necessary skills to know how to get the very best out of every member of staff, then arrange to attend a management training course or speak with one of your mentors about this.

Three key responsibilities that all successful managers possess are that they oversee all areas of leadership, learning and management within an organization. They want the employees they manage to choose to follow them, rather than feel as though they are being forced into anything they don't want to do. It's being able to motivate and encourage employees within their division.

There are certain things that effective managers know how to do in order to achieve maximum results:

- Allow individual team members the opportunity to share their ideas—giving everyone an equal opportunity to say what they want to say and recognizing them for their input.

- Assess each employee's strong points and assign them tasks and duties in line with these.

- Direct individuals toward the purpose behind activities.

- Motivate and encourage them in such a way that it brings out the best in them.

- Reprimand staff in private and recognize and reward them openly.

- Take accountability for the failures of a team, but recognize the team's contributions to the successes.

View each member of staff as an individual whose contribution matters.

Different Management Styles

There are many different management styles that are currently recognized. Here are some that are regularly referenced:

Visionary—focuses on motivation of employees, ensuring everyone is headed in the same direction. These managers are also referred to as charismatic, authoritative, and inspirational. Most are extroverts rather than introverts. They are comfortable being under the spotlight. Change managers and those who are willing to take risks make great visionary managers, e.g. Richard Branson.

Democratic—encourages participation and the sharing of ideas. They inspire staff to contribute so the entire organization is able to benefit from an entire team coming up with solutions to problems, e.g. Google, where the environment is set around equal contribution.

Pacesetter—leads from the front. They can be seen as hard taskmasters. Essentially, what they are doing is challenging their employees to achieve new targets and goals to keep pushing them further and further, e.g. Elon Musk.

The other styles are:

Authoritarian—communicates clearly but directs and controls. This has also been referred to as autocratic and assertive. This type of manager would always have their finger on the pulse of all activity.

Servant—employee centered, also referred to as coaching, supporting, or mentoring. These leaders spend their time working together with their employees. They are mentors, coaches, trainers, and also adept at performing the work their employees do.

Transactional—will negotiate on the basis of employee performance. They will promise performance-based incentives and bonuses. This manager believes greater margins are achieved by the promise of reward that's directly linked to performance.

As a manger you will naturally sway towards one or other of these styles. It is important to know what kind of manager you are in reality and what kind of manager you want to be and understand the steps you need to take to make the jump. You should also consider what type of manager you work best with or under, and try to identify their traits through the interview process.

Prioritization and Effective Delegation

In a world where there is a never-ending demand on our time, it becomes more important than ever before that we figure out how to prioritize and delegate effectively. Being able to prioritize effectively can prevent feelings of being totally overwhelmed and being able to delegate effective can help build successful teams Being able to prioritize not only increases productivity output, but allows one to manage time more effectively as well.

Prioritizing can be as simple as making a list of all the things that you need to do, ranking them in order of importance, and doing them. If only it were actually that simple, we would all be operating on 100% efficiency permanently.

So, here are some of the best ways of being able to prioritize effectively.

Consider everything you regularly do within a month. Put these all into a single master list. Take this list and divide each of these tasks into monthly, bi-weekly, weekly, and daily goals. Your main list will be somewhat of a brain dump.

This is as simple as taking a piece of paper and writing down everything that you have going on in your head. Some of these things can be as simple as phoning someone to wish them happy birthday to clearing out your email inbox. Clear everything out of your head.

Don't worry about how many things are cropping up in your head, that's the whole idea. Write down absolutely everything that is keeping you awake at night or preventing you from focusing properly. You will notice that once everything is written down, your mind will already feel much lighter.

Once you have done this on your master list, divide each activity into daily, weekly, bi-weekly, and monthly tasks. For example, you need to submit a report to management on the last Friday of every month. This should be scheduled into the slot where you know you have all the information necessary to complete this task. Add that to your diary or to-do list for that period. Other tasks such as clearing your emails, delegating tasks, or following up on projects are possibly daily or weekly activities; begin to schedule these in.

At the end of this process, you will discover that you feel more in control of things and what once seemed like a never-ending supply of tasks and challenges is now definitely more manageable.

Delegation is a core difference between being a worker and a manager. It is one that hardworking people feel uncomfortable to adopt. Will they be seen as lazy, will they be caught out in a meeting when would they know the answer if they did it themselves, will someone in the team outshine them? These are concerns you might have, but in truth, they will hold you back. There is no way to successfully be a manager and do all the work yourself. You will begin to suffer from burnout by trying to manage everything on your own.

Delegate wherever possible. You need to be able to let go of some of your responsibilities and begin to trust those of your team. It also provides them with an opportunity to grow and learn new things. Even if they happen to fail, it's still a learning curve for those reporting to you. Some managers make the mistake of holding onto too much without being willing to take a chance on their employees to be able to fulfill assignments.

Managing a team effectively means allowing those reporting to you to fail. That's how we learn and grow. There needs to be an element of trust. They should feel comfortable enough that they know that should they need to, they can approach you with any questions and that if they do fail, you won't dismiss the rest of their contributions but will support them and help steer them back on the right course.

Making Decisions With Your Head and Not Your Heart (Take Emotion Out of the Equation)

As a leader, it's very easy to become emotionally attached and invested in those reporting to you. It is easy to care how others feel. If you didn't care, there would be something wrong with you. You need to be able to make difficult decisions by stepping back and removing emotion from the equation. This doesn't mean losing empathy or not being able to have a human conversation, but it does mean on occasion needing to apply a logic-based approach to a decision first. Once you have made your decision, you can overlay it with the impact it might have on your team. Your next step is to think through how you will communicate your decision and deal with individual reactions. This is a skill that takes some time to master because as leaders we all want to be liked and trusted.

At first this will feel uncomfortable and take some time to think through – don't be afraid to use your mentor, a trusted peer or manager to validate your approach. Over time you will find the decision-making process even for hard or unpopular decisions will come more easily. It takes practice and building up trust in your own judgement and leadership. As a leader, though, it is your responsibility to decide what happens within your division for the collective good of the wider team or organization.

Succession Planning

Every good leader should be grooming and training someone else who can easily fill their shoes whenever the time is right. This involves close mentoring. Choosing a single individual may be putting all your eggs in one basket. You never know what the future holds and they may very well gain the experience from your tutelage and use it as a steppingstone elsewhere. The main aim with succession planning is to have one or two individuals with the right temperament, skills and mindset to be able to take over the reins whenever you are either promoted or leave. It should be remembered that these individuals still need to work as part of their current teams.

Your organization may have a specific way of identifying 'key talent' or 'leadership potential'. They may also have training programs for individuals in these categories. Ask your leader or HR for more information if this isn't clear to you. Know who your potential successors may be and ensure they are set up to succeed by offering exposure to the right situations.

Look at those who are willing to go above and beyond the normal day-to-day requirements as part of the team. Some of this might include job shadowing, attending or deputizing meetings with/for you, and sharing information regarding specific tasks that are required of you as a manager versus what they are currently responsible for now as a part of your team.

Chapter 7: Managing Politics and Influencing Others

"A clay pot sitting in the sun will always be a clay pot. It has to go through the white heat of the furnace to become porcelain."
~ Mildred Struven

In this section we are going to consider office politics and how it affects us and those around us. We'll also touch on ways to deal with it and how to move beyond the position you find yourself in.

What Is Office Politics?

What are some of the first ideas that spring to mind when we use the words "office politics" together to describe the workplace? If you happen to mention gossip, backstabbing, deception or throwing people under the bus to achieve your own agenda, you'd be partially correct.

According to the Merriam-Webster dictionary, office politics is defined as "often disapproving: the activities, attitudes, or behaviors that are used to get or keep power or an advantage within a business or company." The sad part is that it happens in even the best of organizations to varying degrees.

In most instances, office politics does very little to build a team. Instead, the focus is on fracturing relationships through malicious actions that can have devastating consequences in the workplace.

It is possible to succeed solely on merit; however, by avoiding all politics, you are likely to considerably slow your route to the top.

The key point here is to be aware of office politics. This means being conscious of the dynamics between leaders, picking up on informal social clues and understanding in a broader organizational context the direction and relationships of individuals, teams, and divisions.

You should be looking to successfully navigate this minefield. It is ultimately for you to decide how you wish to do this, but our suggestion would be to do so without developing a clear allegiance to any one party. Otherwise, you may find yourself in a very awkward position if they fall out of favor.

How Often Does Office Politics Have an Influence?

It's fair to say that office politics almost always has an influence on the energy within a work environment. Some people seem to have a need to play games with one another. Some are prepared to walk all over anyone who gets in their way (usually without warning). Some of the reasons that individuals may use office politics within an organization are:

- As a means of achieving their goals.

- As a means of seeking approval from management that are more senior than their own.

- Individuals working with their own personal agendas (self-promotion).

- Power play in the sense that they feel the need to be in control. This happens especially in team situations.

- They may be doing it to further their own career aspirations and to block the aspirations of others.

- They try to garner benefits or favor from upper management, often going directly over their own manager's head. This is also to promote themselves into other positions as quickly as possible.

- When those playing the "office politics game" are looking at furthering only their own agenda, they don't really care what the repercussions are going to be or who gets hurt during the process.

Office politics can create dysfunctional decisions which are not made in the best interest of the company, but to further an individual's interest. However, you must consider if you want politics to influence your career or if it is better to influence politics.

If you chose to play the game, be aware it could backfire. Probably up to half your audience will see through this unless you have some substance to support your position.

Managing Stakeholders and Influencing the Decisions/ Outcomes

This usually takes place when vacancies become available within organizations. The higher you go, the fewer top vacancies there are, so this can become a political process. If you know that someone is playing the office politics game, then it is well worth your while to do as much as you can to make yourself known. It is also letting the other party know that you are onto them, rather than allowing them to walk all over you.

This is a skill set that you can develop. You will need to be ready to defend your position as a manager and leader within the organization because you never know if part of the plan is to make you obsolete within the business. This sounds harsh, but it unfortunately does happen.

Making Your Presence Felt

Just as important as doing a good job, is making sure that your presence as a team player is recognized and your contribution doesn't go unrecognized. Unfortunately, even the best staff members can be under-recognized by leadership as the message doesn't get to them or gets absorbed as a team effort, so you need to be willing to do a little bit of self-promotion even if it makes you feel uncomfortable or you are naturally a humble person.

To give an example from my experience, I once had two managers over a period of around five years. The first was the reason I joined the company, and I thought I'd learn from him the most. He was incredibly clever, but was very focused to improve himself and further his own career. He ended up being a highly successful CEO, but at the time, he had no interest in sharing my contribution, only his own promotion. When he left, I had to pick up the pieces of an abandoned project and support a new manager coming in. That manager, while technically not as capable, was much more willing to share the praise for the successes of the team, and while I worked hard for him, he made sure I was recognized for the work.

For me, the second manager was a much better manager to work for and helped me to understand the importance of self-promotion. Incidentally, that manager has had an equally successful career. I understand the first manager found his feet and is much better as a leader now.

The knowledge from that role with my second manager helped me to understand how to market myself with other key stakeholders, helped me to achieve six promotions in the subsequent five years.

Gaining experience and expertise within this realm of business can definitely strengthen you. There are specific areas that you need to be aware of when it comes to office politics, and this is where being forewarned is being forearmed and ready for action.

Some of the main reasons why people even engage in office politics are:

- Achieving their own personal goals and objectives above those of the company.

- Going after promotions or other vacancies before openings are even announced. This is done by making passes at executive managers to lobby their cause directly to them.

- Influencing others to join them in the form of alliances, or groups who potentially have the same or similar vision.

- Power plays—they are hungry to make power within the business their own.

- Promotion of their own ideas for the organization.

- Insecurity – individuals early on in their career may mistake engaging in office politics for being aligned to a 'tribe' who provide them with security and organizational protection. In reality this is rarely the case.

While not everyone is interested in these petty power struggles, they often get sucked in either due to their gentle nature or being hot-headed. You can imagine that these two different personalities are complete polar opposites from one another. You need to be prepared to deal with and dispense with these battles from the moment they indicate they are likely to move into a power play situation.

Making Politics Work for You

The big question is, how do you make politics work in your favor? You can flip office politics on its head completely by:

- Forming alliances—choose to partner up with those who think exactly the same way as you do. This will take some of the sting out of this advancement in an attempt to get what they want.
- Choose your friends wisely and then watch them. When you have formed alliances, remain true to them and whoever else you decided to choose.
- Beware of negative vibes, especially in the workplace. You will find that within a relatively short space of time, negativity can develop, causing a toxic work environment. Choose to let this negativity go.

One thing you may very well find as part of your office politics experience is others taking or attempting to take credit for your work. To save yourself from this, it's recommended you keep copies of everything you do and ensure that others have visibility of your progress.

Communicate with your superiors as to what is happening with your work, any particular projects you're working on, and so on. This is to keep them updated, but has the additional consequence of not allowing anyone else to take the credit for your achievements.

Using Politics to Accelerate Your Career

While this tactic is often used in the world of business to accelerate your career, it is not always seen as the right way of going about things. You don't have to use underhand methods, or take credit for the work of others in order to progress

By all means, make yourself known to management, but go about it in the right way. You want to be noticed and respected, not recognized as an individual that divided a department because of malicious or selfish actions. No matter how well-intentioned you may believe these attempts are, in most situations they are extremely destructive and may damage your own career.

There's a right way and a wrong way to influence the decisions of others. Focus on learning how to go about things the right way, earning people's respect and demonstrating your ability to add value to your role or organization's goals.

Chapter 8: The Leap to the Boardroom

"Before you are a leader, success is all about growing yourself. When you become a leader, success is all about growing others."
~Jack Welch

The truth is that the leap to the board room isn't as huge as many think and comes to most like a natural evolution rather than a leap. If you have served your dues, most of the lessons will have been learned organically. By the time you are in the boardroom, you will be well established as a manager, but you may not be recognized throughout the organization as a leader.

In this penultimate section, we are going to look at the major differences between management and leadership, as well as ways to hone your skills to become the best leader possible.

Moving From Management to Leadership

There's a huge difference between managing people and actually leading people. How will you know when you've successfully transitioned between the two? This is a common question that managers often have to ask themselves. Here are some of the main differences:

- A manager has a myopic view of the individuals they are responsible for. It's people-centric rather than outcome-centric.

- A manager looks at how much output can be achieved within a certain amount of time; a leader looks at adding additional value to the output of the team they're responsible for.
- Managers delegate and have power over their subordinates. Leaders, on the other hand, work with their circle of influence. The litmus test for this is paying specific attention to how many people within the organization ask you for advice without them reporting to you.

There's a major difference between managing workflow through your department and leading people toward the achievement and attainment of goals. It's not about the stick and the carrot in front of the donkey. Instead, this is being able to successfully influence teams. Managers talk about things like what needs to be done, who is responsible for doing it, who will report on it, and so on. A great leader, on the other hand, can flip this entirely on its head and chooses to discuss aspirations, purpose, and the values and vision of the organization instead. Just by doing this, one can see immediately whether the individual is going to be successful as a leader or not.

Leadership Characteristics

The main difference between managing and leading people is that when you are managing them, they are effectively working for you. A leader, on the other hand, creates a group of followers. The manager deals with administrative issues and situations, while the leader works with concepts and visionary requirements.

Leaders often possess the following characteristics:

- They can inspire and motivate others to get to the big picture vision.

- Communication skills are high on their skill set. It's also a key tool that they use when working with those under them.

- Honesty and integrity form the cornerstone of who they are.

- They are long-term, big-picture thinkers rather than only being able to see short-term goals and objectives. A leader needs to be interested in more than just the day job. They need to demonstrate a passion for the business that is inspirational internally and externally, e.g. by representation on external panels.

- They have a vision for the future of the business or organizational objectives.

- They will often inspire out-of-the-box thinking rather than doing things the same way they've always been done.

- They can quickly absorb information and recall relevant facts to make informed and decisive actions. As a manager, it is often difficult to make a decision due to committees etc. A leader's authority can often cut through the red tape.

Managers, on the other hand, are responsible for the day-to-day running of operational requirements. It is much more hands-on and works with policies, procedures, processes, and people.

Executive Responsibilities

By the time that you step into this role, you should be ready for the entire responsibility of all the strategic aspects of any business organization. It's more than simply managing people; a CEO needs to drive the entire business. Accountability for all areas of the business rests on their shoulders. Irrespective of the type of business and industry the organization is in, the CEO remains responsible for the bottom-line earnings and overall profitability of the business.

They are also responsible for developing the vision of the organization, as well as the mission. They must drive the business towards the achievement of goals that have been identified by all management and key stakeholders as being worthwhile.

They are responsible for strategic management and the direction that the business takes. This could include looking for new opportunities, new markets and areas where there are gaps in the marketplace that can potentially be filled. They work in consultation with other executive directors and managers within each of the different divisions to ensure the vision of the organization is upheld.

Part of the CEO's responsibility is to create an environment within the business where employees can meet their targets and objectives, as well as their personal career aspirations.

They are constantly on the lookout for ways to improve systems, processes, policies and procedures. All employees within an organization would take the lead from the CEO by watching them closely and copying their behavior. While not everyone aspires to be a CEO, there are many within the lower echelons of business who have their eyes set on this as their single, most important movement.

For most CEOs, their list of responsibilities is largely dependent on the size of the business, the number of employees, and also the industry that the business operates within and any necessary regulation.

All policies, procedures, and other strategic documents are developed by the CEO in close cooperation with the various divisional directors. It is the CEO's responsibility to take charge and physically lead the entire business organization into the direction they would like it to go.

The CEO gets to meet with all directors within the business organization, as well as the board of directors. During these meetings, overall performance is discussed and reviewed, and targets are set for monthly, quarterly, and annual achievement.

The CEO, in consultation with the finance division, is responsible for all budgets and ensuring that the business remains profitable at all times. This may mean adjusting certain budgets upward and other budgets downward. There are a number of budgets that the CEO would be directly involved with, especially the Capital Expenditure (CAPEX)—these are investments for the future, and the Operating Expenditure (OPEX) budgets—these are day-to-day items (sales and day-to-day costs). If you visualize each budget and each line item within an organization, the CEO is ultimately responsible for deciding whether to keep manufacturing and/or producing certain items that are either obsolete or running at a loss. A CEO has to make decisive and timely decisions that will likely affect the livelihoods of thousands of people.

I recall once being in a meeting with one of the strongest CEOs I've worked with. It was after two periods of losses from an overseas division, and he came to the conclusion that there was no way to fix that business and we needed to put it into an immediate runoff.

For many, this would have appeared like a very tough response to a fairly short period of bad performance and put approximately 100 people out of a job, but he had joined together a lot of dots from the sales, operations, finance, HR, and technical teams to arrive at the conclusion to fix it would cost more than could ever be the reward from that business. By making a sharp decision he saved the business the best part of $20 million in further losses, but in the lead-up to that decision, he was open to listening to everyone's views before finalizing his own.

The entire bottom line is the CEO's responsibility, and while they may not be responsible for all the sales and marketing that happens within the organization, they are certainly responsible to the shareholders for generating a return.

CEO's therefore have a vested responsibility for all operations, ensuring that targets are met or exceeded. They not only set the benchmark for the business, but the buck stops with them when things go wrong.

As an executive you need to accept and understand that any new recruits are going to always look to you as a role model. They will take the lead from you. From the way you carry yourself, the way you interact at all levels of the organization, the way you behave within and outside the business organization, even down to the way you dress—there is always someone who is constantly watching you. Sounding kind of creepy right?

Leadership characteristics don't just happen magically overnight; if so, all companies and organizations the world over would be perfect. We know that this is an impossibility, so what is the next best thing for you as a leader? Being honest, there isn't a clear answer to this question. There are many different types of leaders, some theorists even try to label them, but you just need to be conscious of how your personality impacts the way you lead. Also, remember, leading and managing are two vastly different things. Many leaders struggle manage well, but they typically are great role models and motivators.

Crisis Management

This is being able to manage any threat to the business, whether internal or external, in such a way that substantial loss is avoided. Examples of external threats could be from competitor price slashing, competitors poaching teams, pandemics or financial markets sliding into a depressed or recessionary state. Internal threats could include burglary, fire, or anything untoward happening directly within the physical structure of the business.

The correct way for handling crisis management is to get on top of it as quickly as possible to minimize the potential fallout as a result of the event and is where a CEO earns their reputation. Areas within the organization that could experience potential threats include finance, the reputation of the business and the health and safety of employees.

There's a big difference between crisis management and handling a crisis once it has occurred. The actual crisis management is a policy or strategy that's put in place to minimize risk in the event of an unforeseen crisis happening within the organization. On the other hand, once a crisis occurs, the time comes to implement the crisis management strategy to try to minimize the overall impact on the business.

Understanding Your Industry Influence, LinkedIn, Attending Events as a Speaker, Blogs

Your industry potentially has a huge impact on the way things are run. You can make it stand out even further by making use of various tools out there to promote your business. One of these is LinkedIn. Companies are making use of this platform daily to connect with like-minded individuals, suppliers, and potential customers. There are community forums where you can contribute written articles to get noticed or upload videos to inform those in your industry of some of the things that are happening specifically with your business.

Another idea is to run a regular blog that connects directly through to your social media channels. Blogs can be anything from informative to entertaining. Remember to always play to your specific target audience and maximize your exposure to benefit your business as much as possible.

Chapter 9: Defining Your End Game

"Try and leave this world a little better than you found it and when your turn comes to die you can die happy in feeling at any rate you have not wasted your time but have done your best."
~ Baden Powell

Sculpting Your Legacy

As you consider the legacy you would like to leave behind, think about the choices and decisions you're making now. It's choosing to always show up, being both dependable and reliable. It's choosing to live your life according to set standards of integrity, honesty, and humility while still remaining true to who you are. Sculpting a legacy means taking the time to actively engage in your current role to the very best of your ability so you can leave an indelible mark on the world.

When you hear the word legacy, your mind is often sent in the direction of what you're leaving behind for future generations. In business, however, this is somewhat different. You are looking at leaving a strong enough business with such a solid foundation that the business continues to grow and prosper long after you have stepped down, retired, or handed over the reins to another CEO. What type of mark are you leaving within your sphere of influence, whether that's a team, business, community or world?

If you aren't certain of what message you want to leave within your business or on the world in general, you may need to take some introspective time on your own to decide on what you plan to leave behind. It might be something you discuss with a mentor or coach. This is something that you will always be remembered for. It's your specific contribution toward the business organization and the mark that you want to leave.

The business and economic environment is always changing, that is no secret. The big question is, as a CEO within this ever-morphing environment, how are these changes going to influence you, the people you're responsible for managing, and how and where are you able to change your business to meet the new global landscape that has become the world of work? What are you as the CEO prepared to do to make those bold changes to impact the world?

An example of this is when Mary Barra was made the very first female CEO of General Motors International. Some of the decisions she made were initially controversial. Her recalling a massive number of vehicles to ensure they were safe on the road and preventing as much reputational damage as possible was not always seen as the most commercial move at the time. However, once management and others within the organization could see the benefit in why she was doing this, they were able to stand behind her decision.

While still climbing the corporate ladder and working in HR, Mary also amended the massive corporate dress code policy document from 20+ pages down to a single sentence: "Dress appropriately." Her reasoning behind it was that most of the individuals within the business were responsible for hundreds of thousands of dollars' worth of stock, equipment, budgets, and so on, only to be given very specific instructions on a dress code. This highly simplified policy in two words said it succinctly and created a cultural shift towards one where individuals were more focused on how they did their role and what they achieved rather than mandating what they wore and when. So, you see that legacy actions can be taken in all areas of the organization and at many different levels.

What Culture Can You Adopt?

Just consider how we are currently working in the world right now. One of the biggest questions on anyone's lips is whether we will ever find ourselves returning to the way that things were before 2020. There have been dramatic shifts, not only in how you perceive your role in this new work environment, but in being able to communicate this to your people and having them follow you as far as you want to go. Especially within corporate environments, there has been significant cultural shifts in the last few years and typically they have been positive shifts. Inclusion and diversity has shot up to the top of the agenda for most large multinational organizations, leading to workplaces being adapted to better serve the breadth of the employee base. By joining an organization, you're buying into their culture and you will be responsible for positively adding to that culture.

Understanding What You Want in Your Future

What do you want your future to look like? There are and have been some great leaders whose lives you are about to try to emulate. Where do you see yourself going now that you have reached the top rung of the corporate ladder? All successful leaders constantly have goals that they're working toward at any given time. More importantly, what will be your message to the world, or the world of work? Are you content to go day by day following other market leaders, just keeping your finger on the pulse of whatever is happening out there, or is it time to step up and out of your comfort zone? Questions you should be asking yourself include, "Will the decisions I make today really have an impact on future leaders and the world in general in 10 years' time?"

Decide for yourself what your next step will be/ Are you currently satisfied with where you are in your career, or do you still have some goals that you haven't achieved yet? If you can, identify each of these and write them down. Set your sights on actively working to turn your dreams into a reality.

Work Life Balance

For peace, harmony, and happiness, everything needs to remain in balance. This is especially true when it comes to your work-life balance. Despite the drive and motivation to achieve great things, leaving your mark on your industry may be your immediate focus. There is a reason why you happen to be in the business you are in right now. Only you know what your personal and professional goals are. This is what should drive you to write a new narrative in your industry as a market leader and possibly a global player.

Consider utilizing mindfulness techniques such as self-meditation. Try to find 10 minutes a day for introspection. How are you feeling today? Are you making sensible decisions, or is something playing on your mind? Do you feel in control, or do you need to realize that there are items that are outside of your control? In the heat of work and life it's often difficult to take one step back to realize what is actually important, but utilizing these techniques can better your odds!

When Will You be Satisfied With Where You Are in Your Career?

A pretty important question is whether we ever reach a point in our lives and in our careers where we can honestly say that we are satisfied. If you feel that you are, then consider each of the following questions to confirm this for you.

- Do you feel that you have accomplished everything you've set out to achieve?

- Are there areas of personal growth you think you still need to master? If so, what are these and how can you get there?

- Have you accomplished all your leadership goals?

- What lessons have you specifically learned on this journey from start to CEO?

- If there were some things that you could do differently, what would these be and why?

Where do you see yourself going from here, moving forward?

Starting Your Own Business

You may have decided to venture out on your own after having gained as much exposure as you possibly can within large corporate environments. Understand that there are major differences between working for large corporations versus venturing out on your own. You run the sole risk, reward, and responsibility as to whether your business will succeed.

Depending on the nature of the business, you may well need to hire staff to work with you and assist you in getting the business off the ground. This will necessitate a full risk assessment, considering financials. Do you actually have sufficient capital to be opening this business? Do you have a completed business plan? Are your ideas solid?

Can your business fill a gap in the market? This

information can be determined by undertaking a basic Strengths, Weaknesses, Opportunities, and Threats (SWOT) analysis. Is it sustainable? You always need to look at a business opportunity in the long term. Is it a short-term, quick in and out of the market where you can make a substantial amount of money before getting out? Or is this something that you see yourself doing permanently from here on out?

Before you go into business on your own, you need to be fully aware of all the risks that are involved. Don't lose yourself in a business that is going to drain you mentally, physically, and emotionally without providing the financial rewards at the end of the day.

Investing, Side Hustles, Passive Income and Entrepreneurialism

At the start of your career, most people battle to survive on their current income alone. There are hundreds of thousands of side hustles that you can become involved in, from running an online business to delivering pizzas, driving an Uber, and so on.

There is an unfortunate truth that most people spend as much as they earn. By the time you retire, even a multimillionaire may be in a precarious state where their expenditures exceed their income.

By the time you come to the end of your career, most would hope to no longer be living paycheck to paycheck and have built a substantial portfolio of interest and assets that support your lifestyle. Note that in this definition, we classify assets as things that will provide you with future wealth. A portfolio of fast cars and boats, while traditionally considered assets, only serve as a future drain to your wealth, so purely for this definition, they are considered liabilities.

So, you may need to think about how to start alternate streams of income. These could include investments such as pension, property, equity in startups in exchange for your experience, YouTube, non-executive appointments, and panels. For some people replacing the day job with these alternative activities also eases the shift from career to retirement as you remain active in your industry.

You may want to set up a YouTube channel where you post on a regular basis. This can eventually be monetized, bringing in passive income. Publish on Amazon for decent financial rewards and returns on an initial investment. It also allows you to get your message to the masses.

Becoming an entrepreneur involves coming up with ideas for business and making them happen. Some of the world's most famous leaders started out as entrepreneurs. You don't need to necessarily have a fancy degree or title to make a success of your life. If you have a strong enough desire, you can do absolutely anything.

There are no guaranteed ways to make continued wealth from these choices, but you should utilize your experience to your advantage, whether that be in discovering a new start-up to support as a venture or utilizing your skilled professional network to support your investments.

Receiving sound advice from a financial advisor or portfolio advisor is a good thing. Just as with your career, you need the best team with you to deliver the best result, but you are in the driving seat. You want to be able to grow your nest egg into something that is more tangible and can assist you with your future. If you aren't seeing growth in your portfolio after a fixed amount of time, you may need to review and re strategize your decisions.

When considering investment options and opportunities, always make certain that you are dealing with a professional who understands investments and has a good track record. You can easily find out this information by speaking with your mentor(s) or asking around in the financial industry. If individuals don't have a great track record, it may be worthwhile to replace them with someone who is really going to work with your portfolio with your very best interests at heart.

In everything you do you should be looking to access a World Class team. For example, if you decide to invest in property, get the best team you can together to handle all your affairs. A lawyer you trust, a builder, architect & plumber who you know will deliver. Recognize that these are assets that differentiate your investment from others and help avoid time consuming and expensive mistakes. It's quite possible that $1000 saved on a legal contract by going on the internet may cost you $300k in legal issues to fix an issue after the event.

Wrap Up

My favorite CEO used to often share his views of work. Once, when he was dealing with people's bonuses, I questioned why he had rewarded one person more than another when they had achieved the same results. He said, "Listen, kid, when I give people a bonus, it's not about what they delivered. It's about how they delivered it" Honestly, I didn't understand his response for a long time.

Since then I've worked with hundreds of people, some clearly had their own agenda where we achieved our short term goal but I would not want to work with again and others who were so admired they would attract talent and make a success of any business they worked in.

You only get one chance to play the game, so make sure you get your real-life education, make a firm choice of how you want to get to your destination... and the type of leader you want to be.

References

BrainyQuote.com. (2019). *Legacy quotes | BrainyQuote*. BrainyQuote; BrainyQuote. https://www.brainyquote.com/topics/legacy-quotes

BrainyQuote.com. (2020). *Management quotes | BrainyQuote*. BrainyQuote; BrainyQuote. https://www.brainyquote.com/topics/management-quotes

Campbell, S. (2018, February 1). *8 Habits of highly successful leaders*. Entrepreneur. https://www.entrepreneur.com/article/308282

Corporate Finance Institute. (n.d.). *Office politics—how to deal with politics in the workplace*. Corporate Finance Institute. https://corporatefinanceinstitute.com/resources/careers/soft-skills/office-politics/

Garvey, J. (2019, July 31). *101 Motivational quotes to engage and inspire employees*. Www.peoplegoal.com. https://www.peoplegoal.com/blog/101-motivational-quotes-for-employees

Gerencer, T. (2019, February 20). *20 situational interview questions and answers to nail your interview*. Zety; Zety. https://zety.com/blog/situational-interview-questions

Gregory, A. (2019, February 28). *How small business owners can build a legacy*. The Balance Small Business. https://www.thebalancesmb.com/how-small-business-owners-can-build-a-legacy-4584697

Heathfield, S. M. (2004, February 28). *Tips for effective management success*. The Balance Careers; The Balance. https://www.thebalancecareers.com/tips-for-effective-management-success-1916728

Heathfield, S. M. (2011, February 4). *What does a chief executive officer (CEO) do?* The Balance Careers; The Balance. https://www.thebalancecareers.com/what-does-a-chief-executive-officer-ceo-do-1918528

Koch, L. (2018, July 31). *Leaving a legacy: Your business' success requires a sustainable-first approach*. Entrepreneur. https://www.entrepreneur.com/article/317632

Kruse, K. (2012, October 16). *100 Best quotes on leadership*. Forbes. https://www.forbes.com/sites/kevinkruse/2012/10/16/quotes-on-leadership/?sh=4abd42652feb

MacKay, J. (2020, May 5). *How to prioritize work: 9 Practical methods when "everything is important."* RescueTime Blog. https://blog.rescuetime.com/how-to-prioritize/

Mariliza Karrera. (2017, May 11). *10 Important benefits of networking*. Careeraddict.com. https://www.careeraddict.com/benefits-networking

Meah, A. (2017, May 12). *35 Inspirational quotes on personal development | AwakenTheGreatnessWithin*. Awaken the Greatness Within. https://www.awakenthegreatnesswithin.com/35-inspirational-quotes-on-personal-development/

Merriam Webster Dictionary. (n.d.). *Definition of office politics*. Www.merriam-Webster.com. Retrieved March 10, 2021, from https://www.merriam-webster.com/dictionary/office-politics

Mettl Blog. (2020, July 17). *Behavior assessment tools: The secret sauce to better talent decisions.* Mettl. https://blog.mettl.com/behavioral-assessment-tools/

Mind Tools Content Team. (2009). *7 Ways to use office politics positively getting what you want without "playing dirty."* Mindtools.com. https://www.mindtools.com/pages/article/newCDV_85.htm

Nayar, V. (2014, August 7). *Three differences between managers and leaders.* Harvard Business Review. https://hbr.org/2013/08/tests-of-a-leadership-transiti

Page, M. (2018). *Top 11 benefits of networking | Michael Page.* Michael Page. https://www.michaelpage.com.au/advice/career-advice/career-progression/benefits-networking

Posey, B. (2019). *What is crisis management?—Definition from WhatIs.com* (I. Wigmore, Ed.). WhatIs.com. https://whatis.techtarget.com/definition/crisis-management

Purcell, G. (2019, March 14). *The top 7 management styles: Which ones are most effective?* Workzone. https://www.workzone.com/blog/management-styles/

Siles, R. (2018). *Definition of project success.* Pm4dev.com. https://www.pm4dev.com/pm4dev-blog/entry/definition-of-project-success.html

Tran, T. (2020, March 11). *Top LinkedIn demographics that matter to social media marketers.* Social Media Marketing

& Management Dashboard. https://blog.hootsuite.com/linkedin-demographics-for-business

Wise Sayings. (n.d.). *Networking sayings and networking quotes | Wise Sayings*. Www.wisesayings.com. Retrieved March 10, 2021, from https://www.wisesayings.com/networking-quotes/

Zhang, L. (n.d.). *30 behavioral interview questions to prep for*. The Muse. https://www.themuse.com/advice/30-behavioral-interview-questions-you-should-be-ready-to-answer

www.ingramcontent.com/pod-product-compliance
Lightning Source LLC
Chambersburg PA
CBHW070649220526
45466CB00001B/360